AF262898

CHIN MUSIC
PRESS

CAROL ISAAK

SEASONS
LAN SU GARDEN

COVER PHOTO
Inscription above the moon doorway:
Listen to the Fragrance

dedicated to:
Daniel John Isaak,
patient and generous

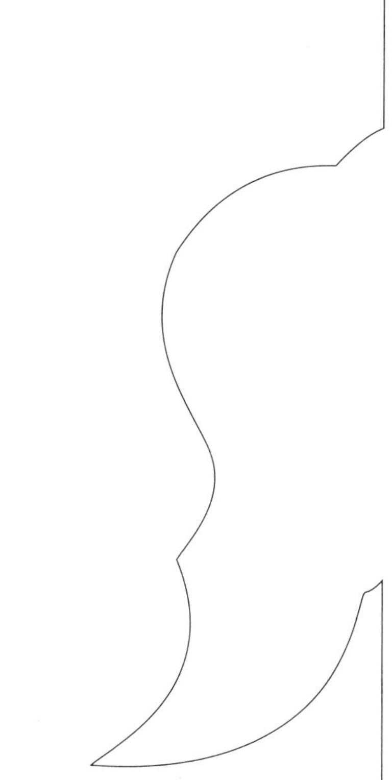

Transformative:
Crossing the threshold
of the Lan Su Garden;
time is suspended.

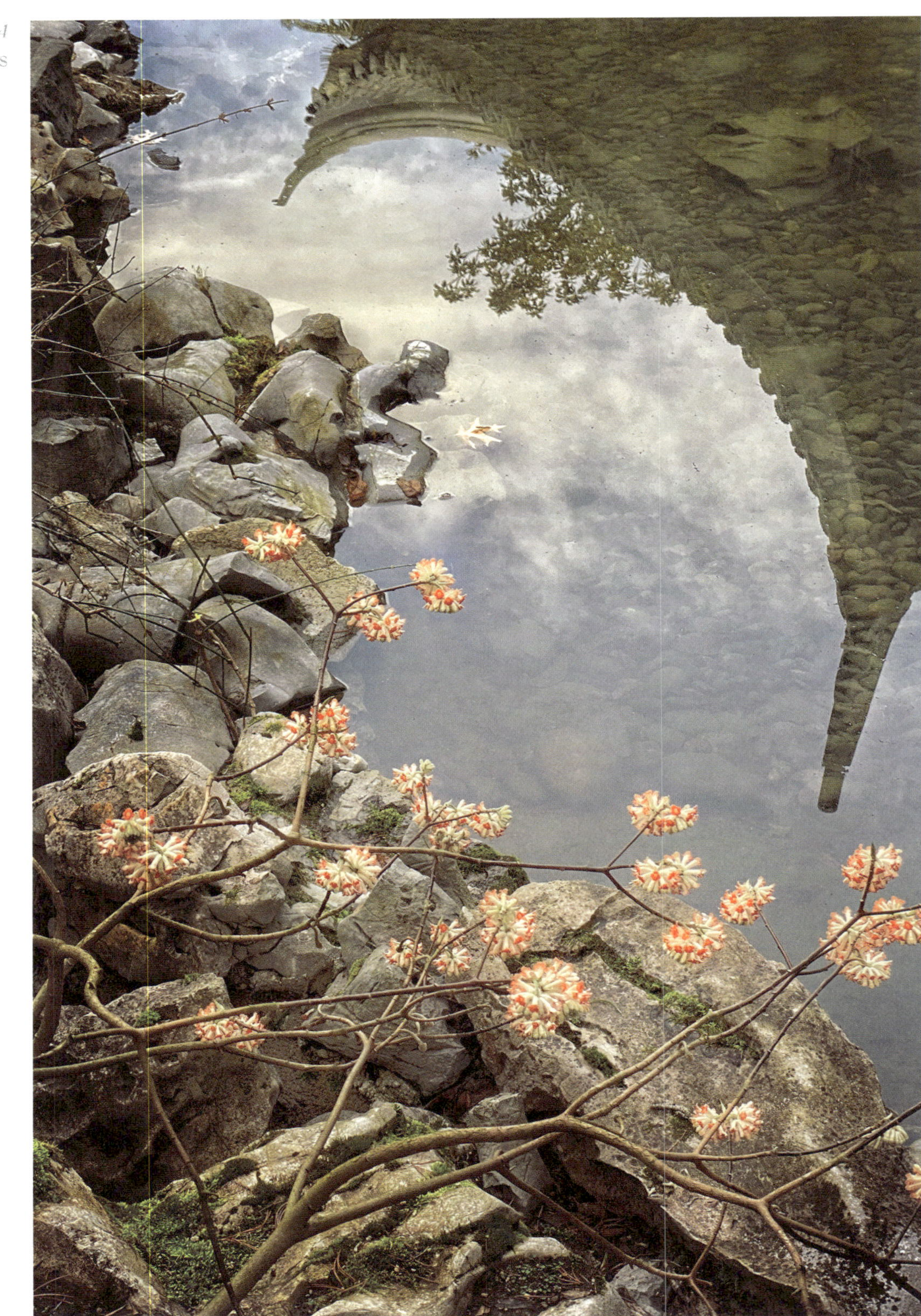

PREFACE

A Journey Through the Seasons of Lan Su Yuan

GLORIA LEE, Opening Executive Director, Lan Su 2000-2008

As we begin the 25th anniversary of Lan Su Yuan, we reflect on the many seasons of man and nature in this oasis of tranquil beauty where plants, rocks, poetry, water, and architecture create a garden for contemplation and solace.

"Most cherished in this mundane world is a place without traffic; Truly in the midst of a city there can be mountain and forest." — Wen Zhengming, 1470-1559. (This inscription is found in a poem located at Flowers Bathing in Spring Rain pavilion.)

This book is a celebration of Lan Su Yuan's seasons, captured through the lens of photography by Carol Isaak. It is an invitation to experience the garden's changing moods as each year unfolds its seasons. Twenty-five years of growth, change, conservation and replenishment continue to reward us in harmonious beauty between nature and humankind.

Each season brings fragrances to delight the senses, blooms to visually inspire, textures from smooth stones to the scholarly Lake Taihu rocks, and the music of mountain water flowing into Lake Zither. Spring brings forth renewal with delicate camellias throughout the garden. Summer brings enlightenment and versatile lotus in Lake Zither. Fall brings the colors of goldfish, koi, and osmanthus. Winter brings perseverance and resilience as the pine, plum, and bamboo stand tall. For every season, Lan Su's covered walkways and architectural pavilions feature drip tiles forming a pearl-like beaded curtain when it rains. On each drip tile are the five blessings: long life, wealth, health, a love of virtue, and a peaceful ending.

Lan Su is a place where one can connect with centuries of Chinese philosophy, art, and storytelling. The winding pathways, the intricate latticework of windows, and the poetic inscriptions that adorn the walls all contribute to a narrative that transcends the seasons. This garden is not merely observed; it is experienced, and each person who walks through its gates finds quiet mindfulness.

Let this book take you on a journey that stretches across the seasons and beyond. Reflect on the beauty that change creates and the mindfulness of living in harmony between humankind and nature.

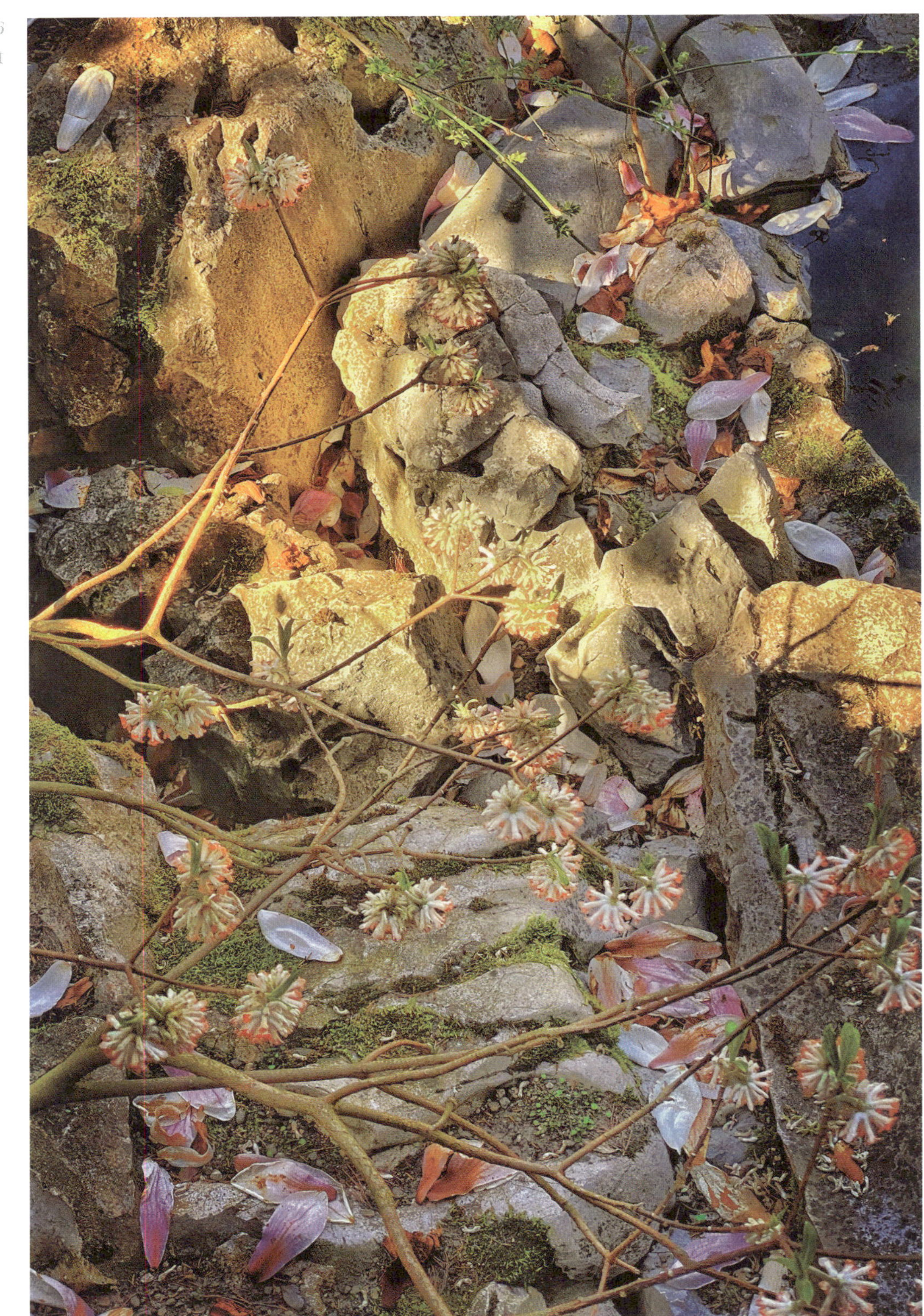

INTRODUCTION

CAROL ISAAK

A refuge of serenity in the middle of Portland, Oregon, the Lan Su Chinese Garden is an escape from the frenetic pace of everyday life. Once you cross its threshold, you are transported someplace else.

Encompassing an entire city block, this white-walled garden is designed to heighten senses but comfort the spirit; to engage the eyes but diminish the rush and tumult.

Built like a fortress, its filigreed exterior walls modulate the light. The structure's interior is divided into spaces that flow one into the other, all opening out into a graciously landscaped exterior space. In the middle of this landscape is an irregularly shaped koi-filled pond.

At the start of the Covid pandemic, and through the present day, I visit the garden many times a week, experiencing the wealth and evolution of each season. As a travel photographer and a lover of things Asian, the garden is my perfect refuge. It requires me to just be. Sometimes the elegant space is full of quiet pleasures and other times the garden is alive with activity.

Koi animate the light-kissed pond, and the reflections in the water all become visual magnets. Abundant plantings embellish the walls and windows. The weathered scholar's rocks, natural sculpture, seduce me. Poetic inscriptions on the walls and stones, full of latent and manifest meaning, weave all these elements together.

To create this oasis, sixty-five craftsmen from Suzhou, China, relocated to Portland, Oregon, their sister city. They worked for nine months constructing this garden. Now, a national treasure, the Lan Su Garden is an authentic design by architect Kuang Zhenyan of a Ming dynasty scholar's retreat.

Through my photographs... enter my refuge with me.

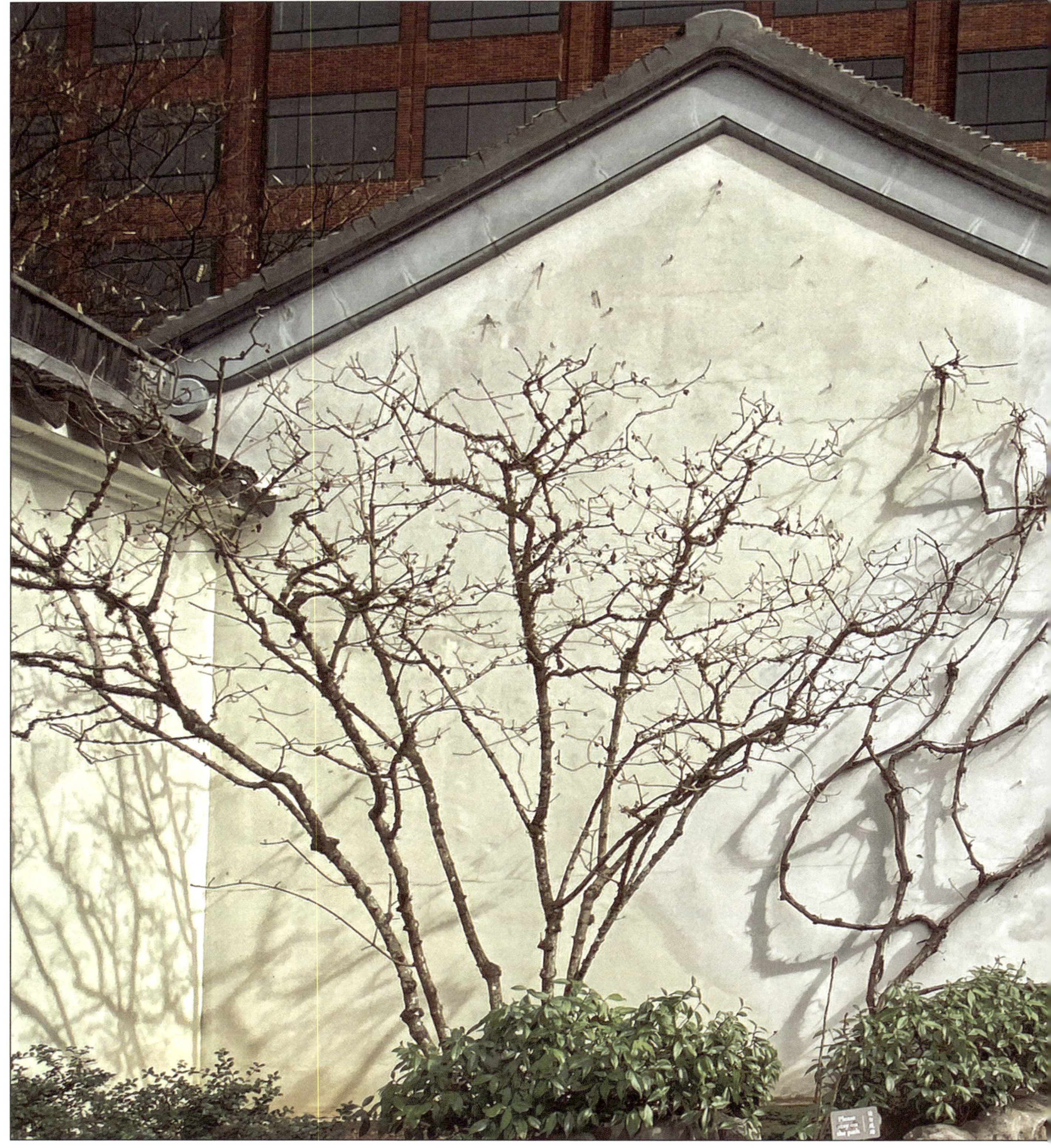

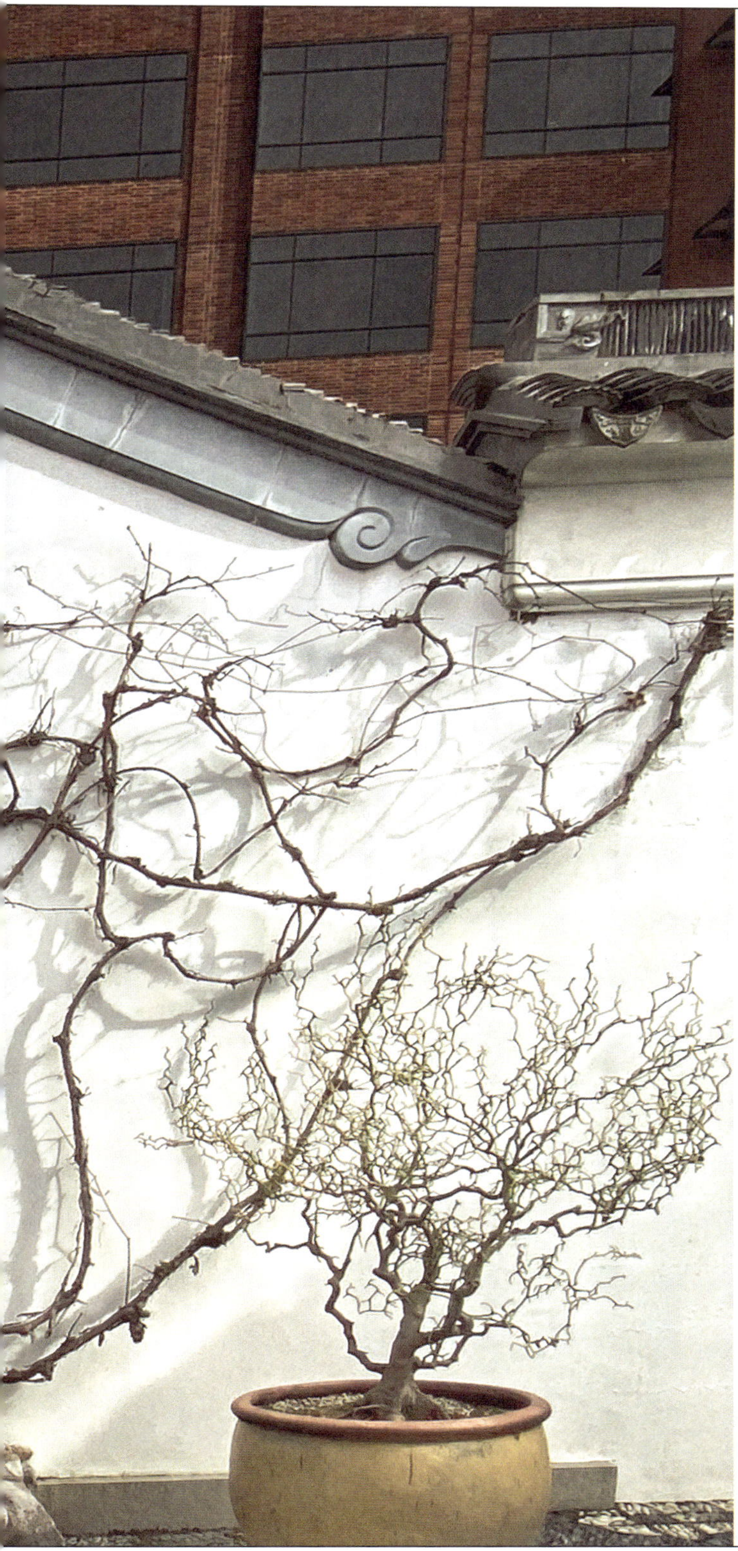

WINTER'S END

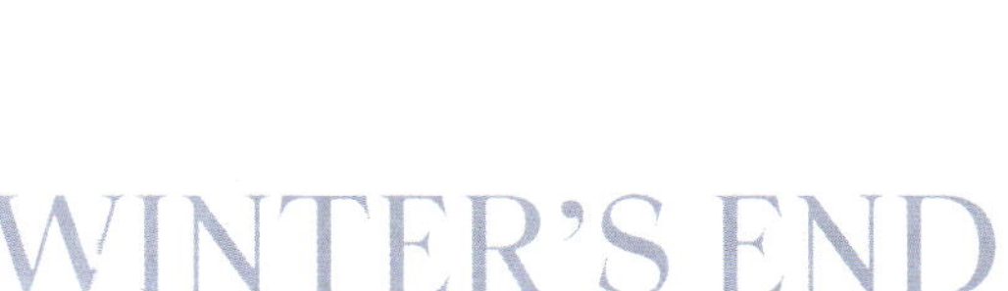

Red lanterns indicate the New Year

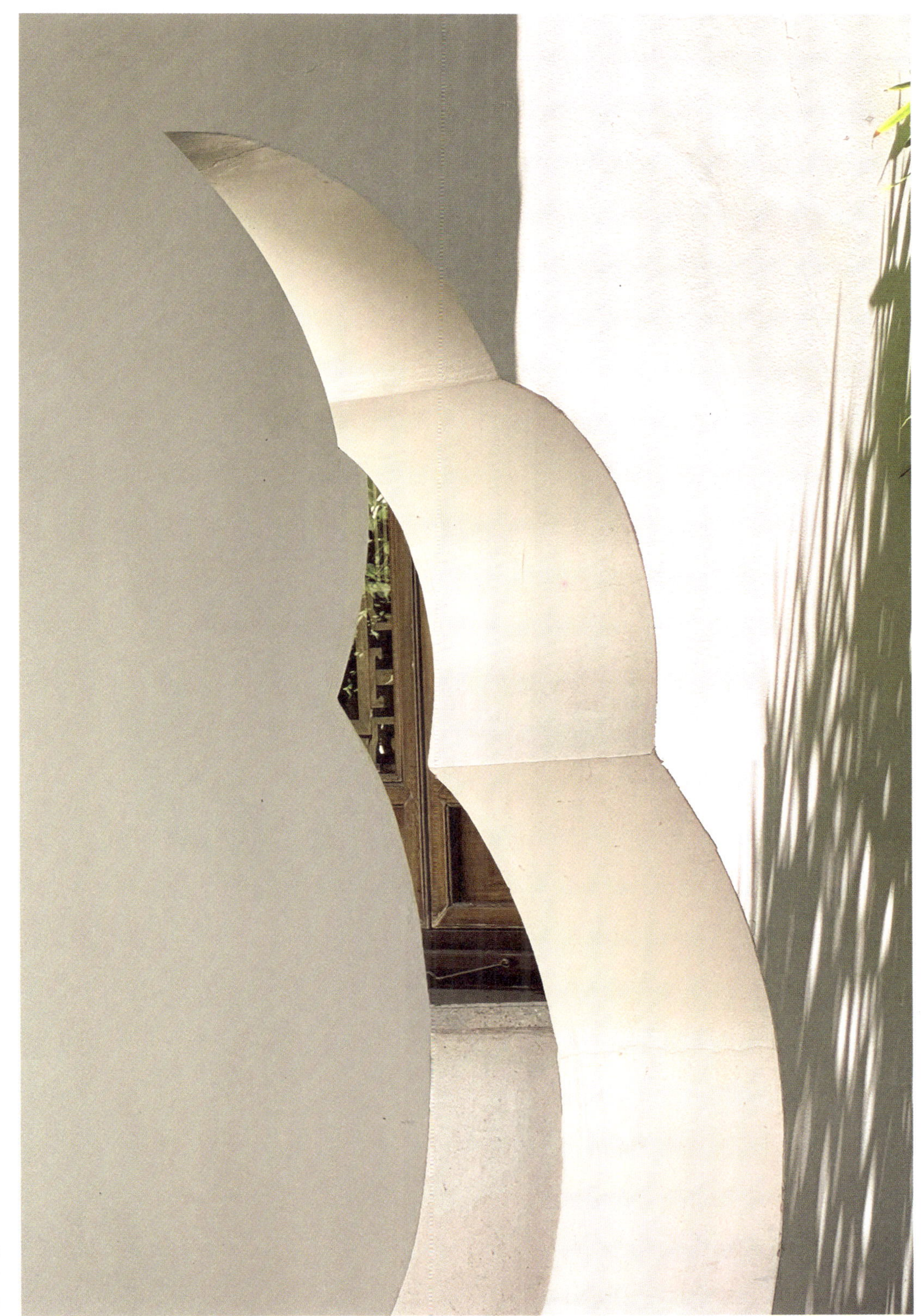

Light Cast Through
Pepper Doorway

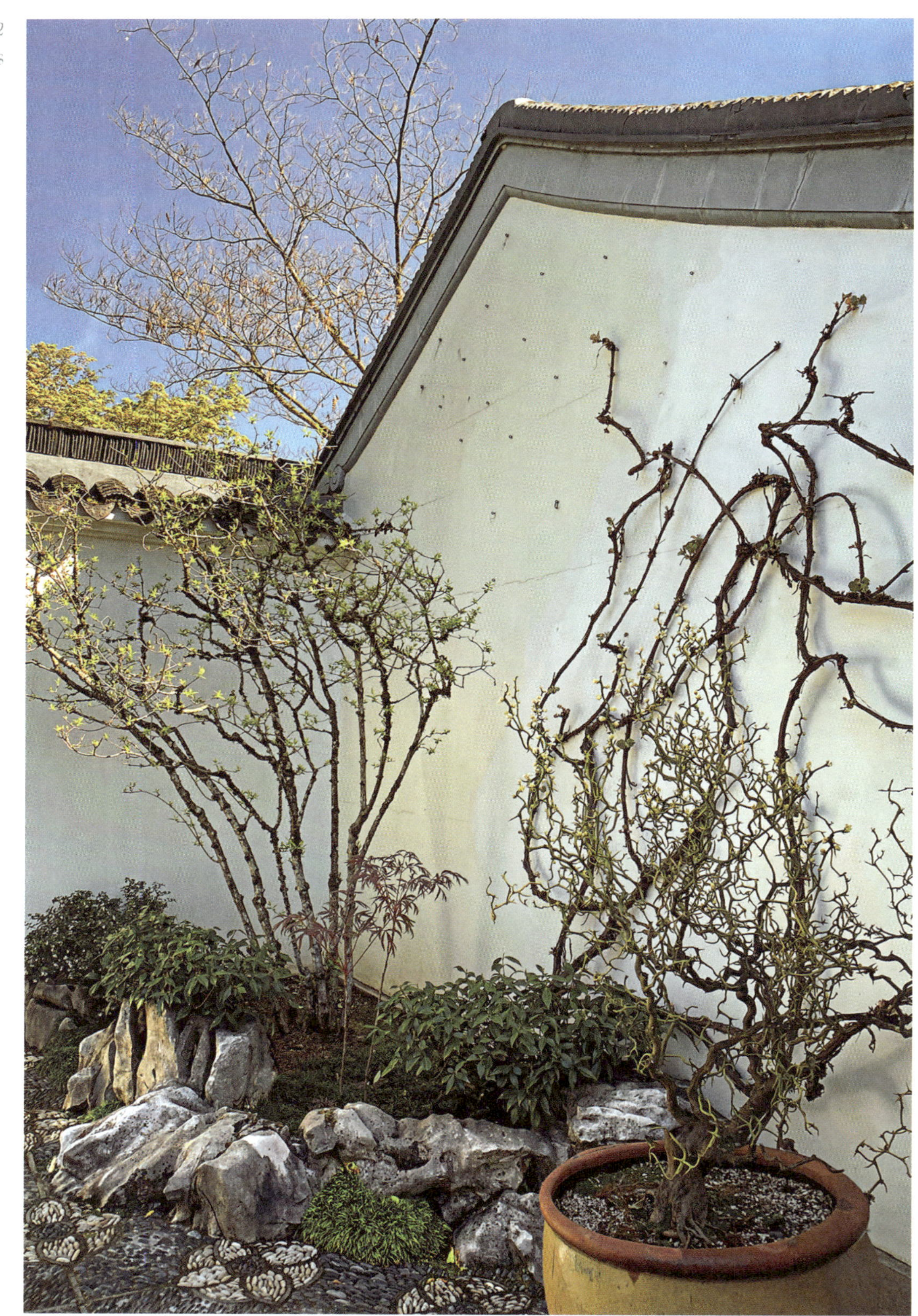

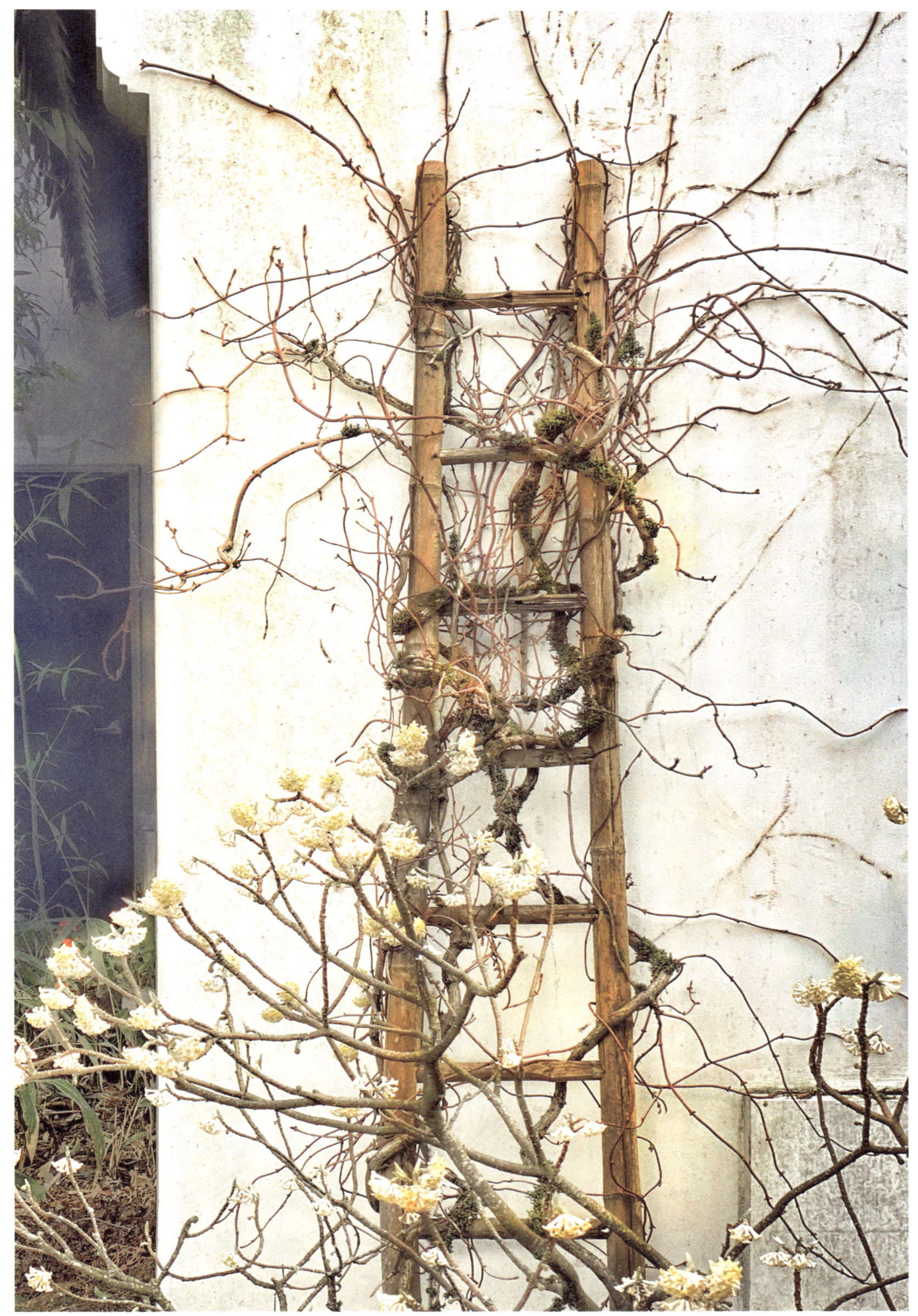

Vines and Ladder

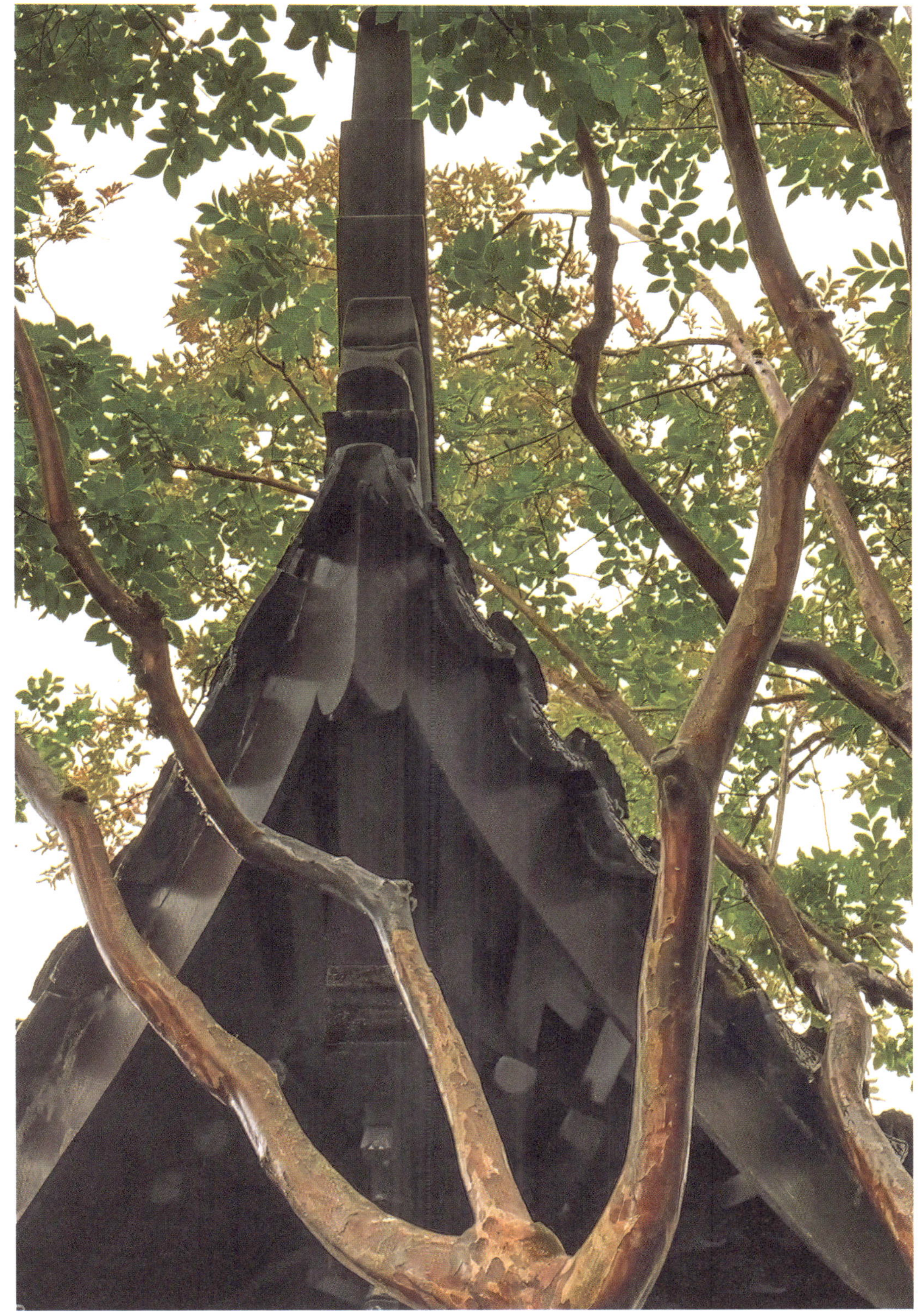

Forked Eave

Bridge and Lanterns

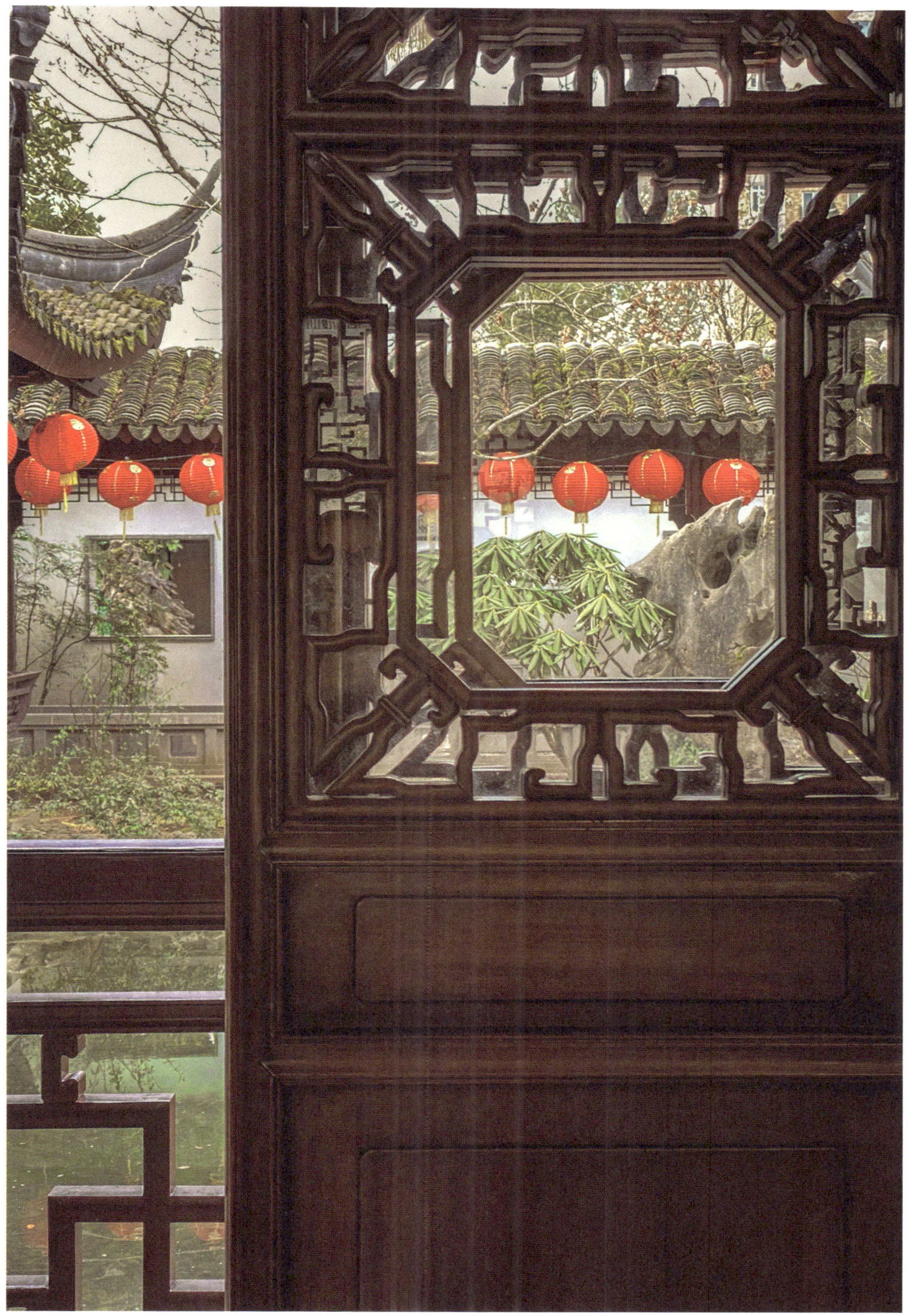

Doorway to Courtyard

17

Rocks with Pool

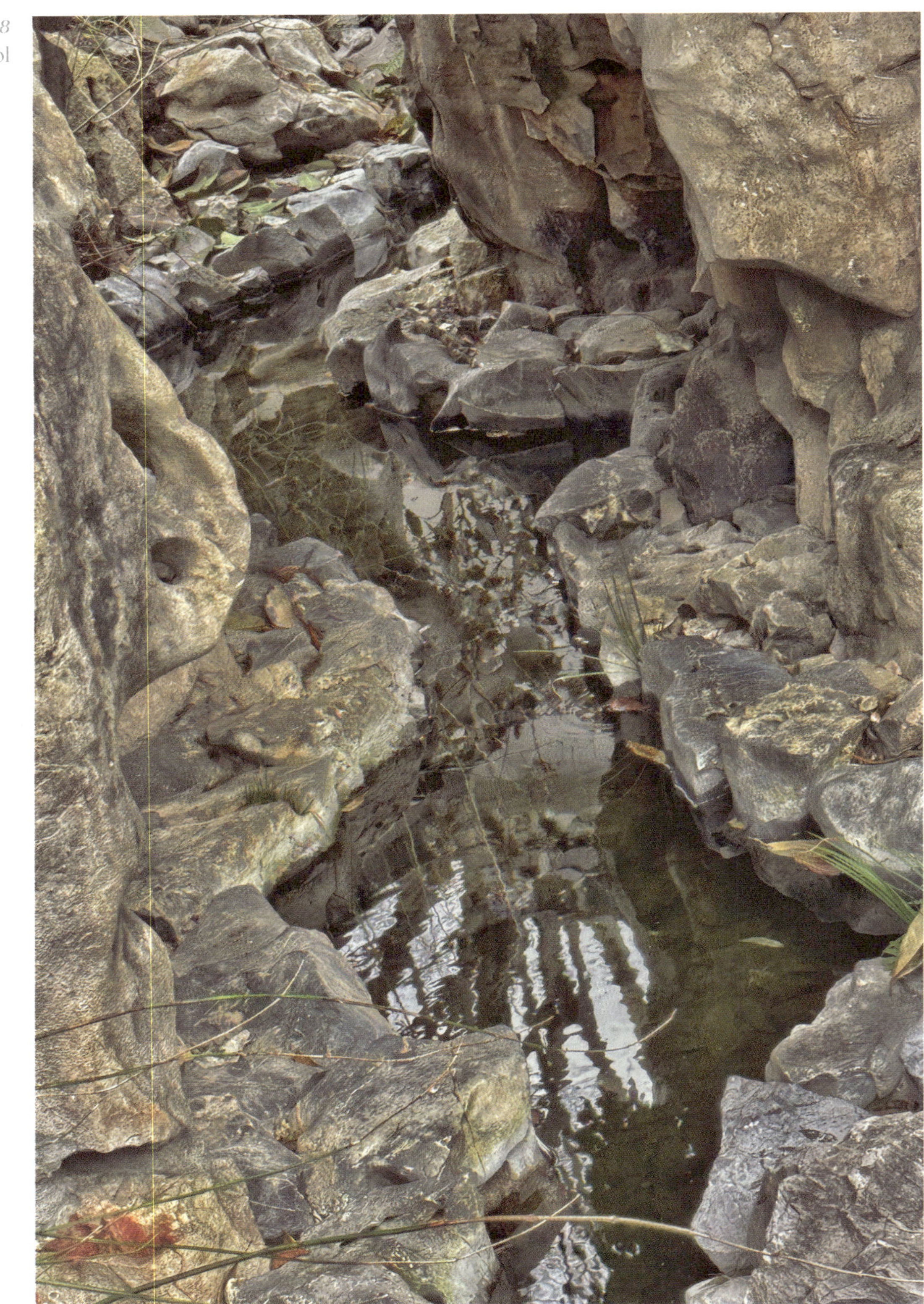

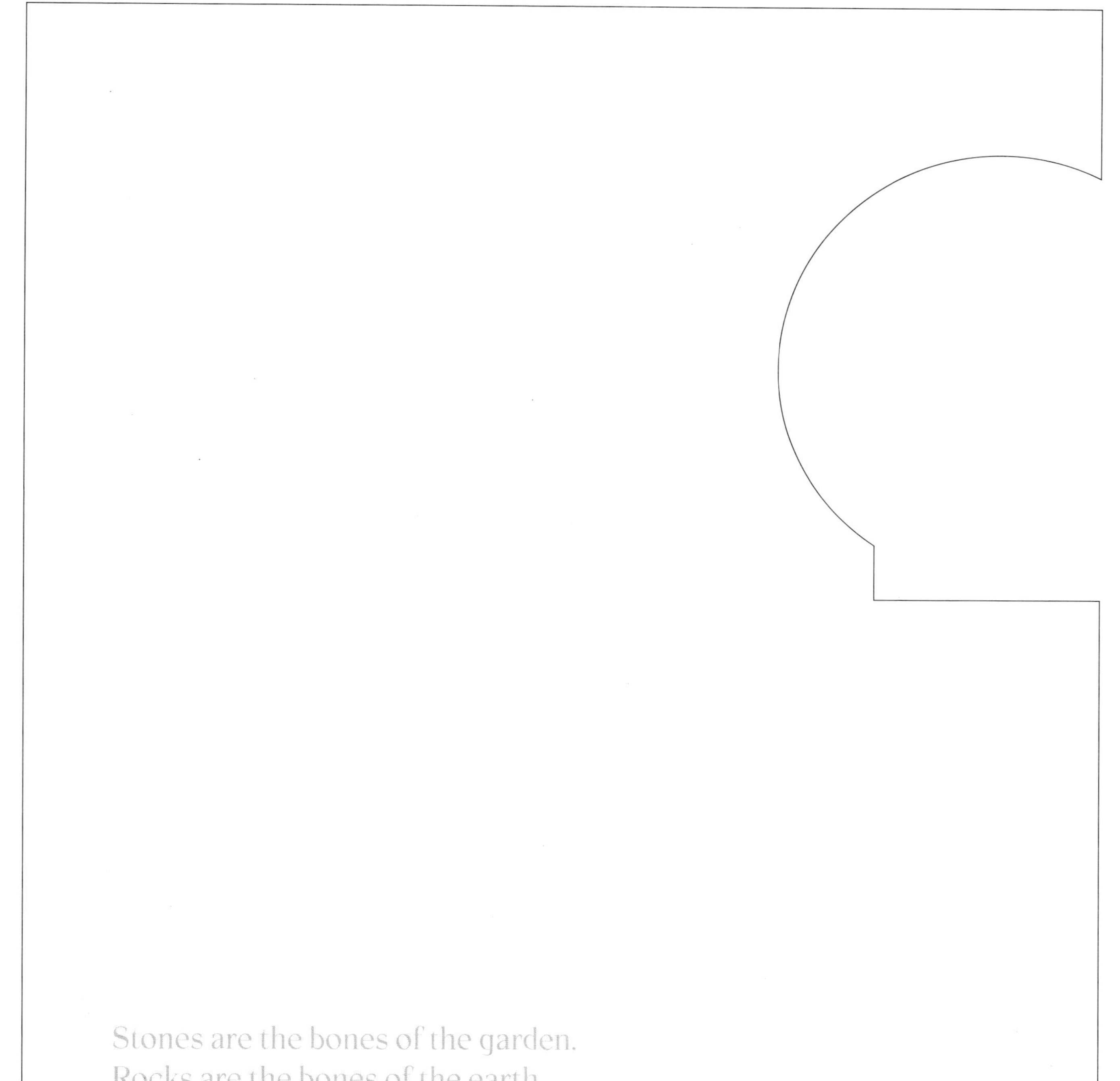

Stones are the bones of the garden.
Rocks are the bones of the earth.
Many formations emerge as mountains.
Water is a life force.

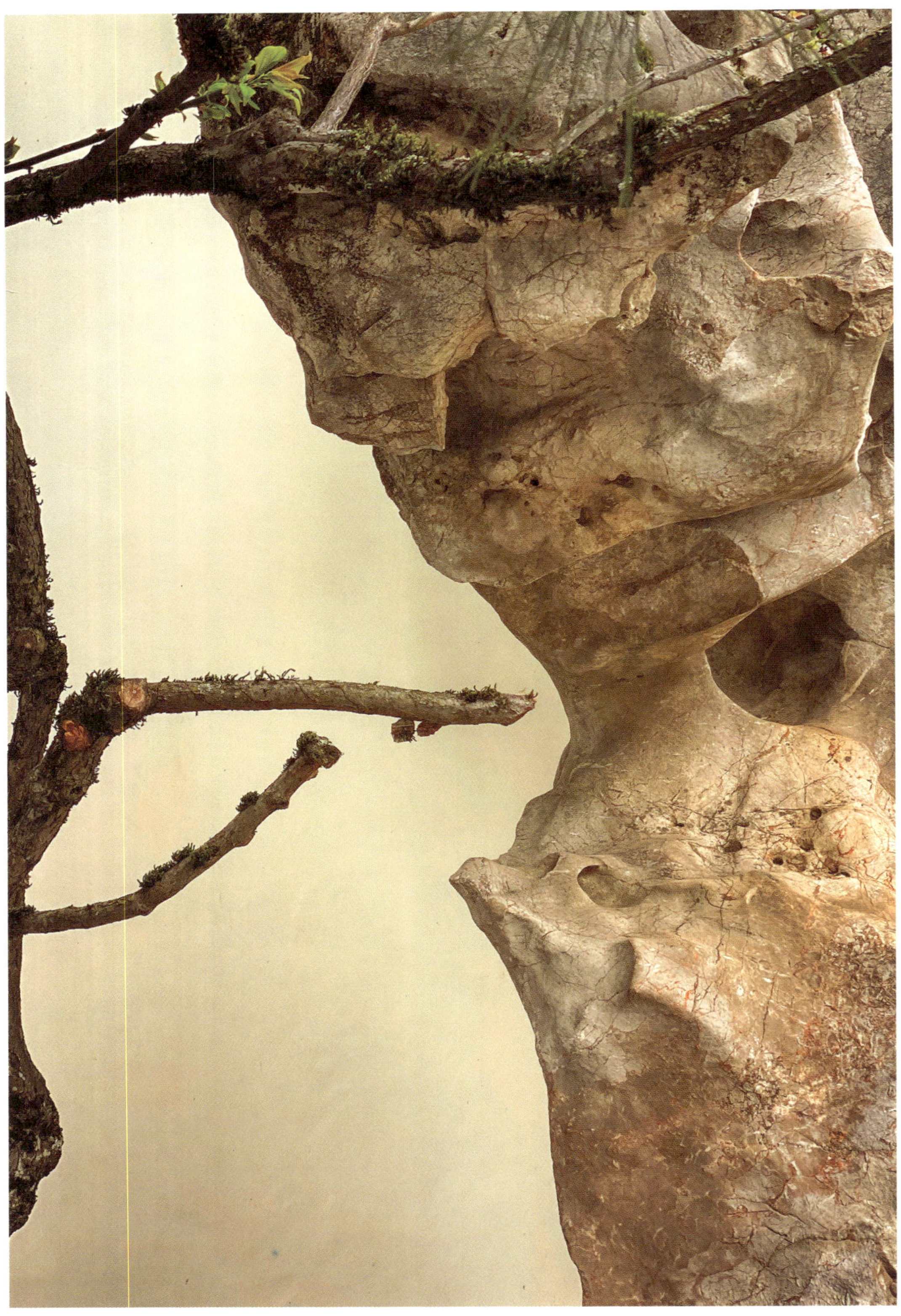

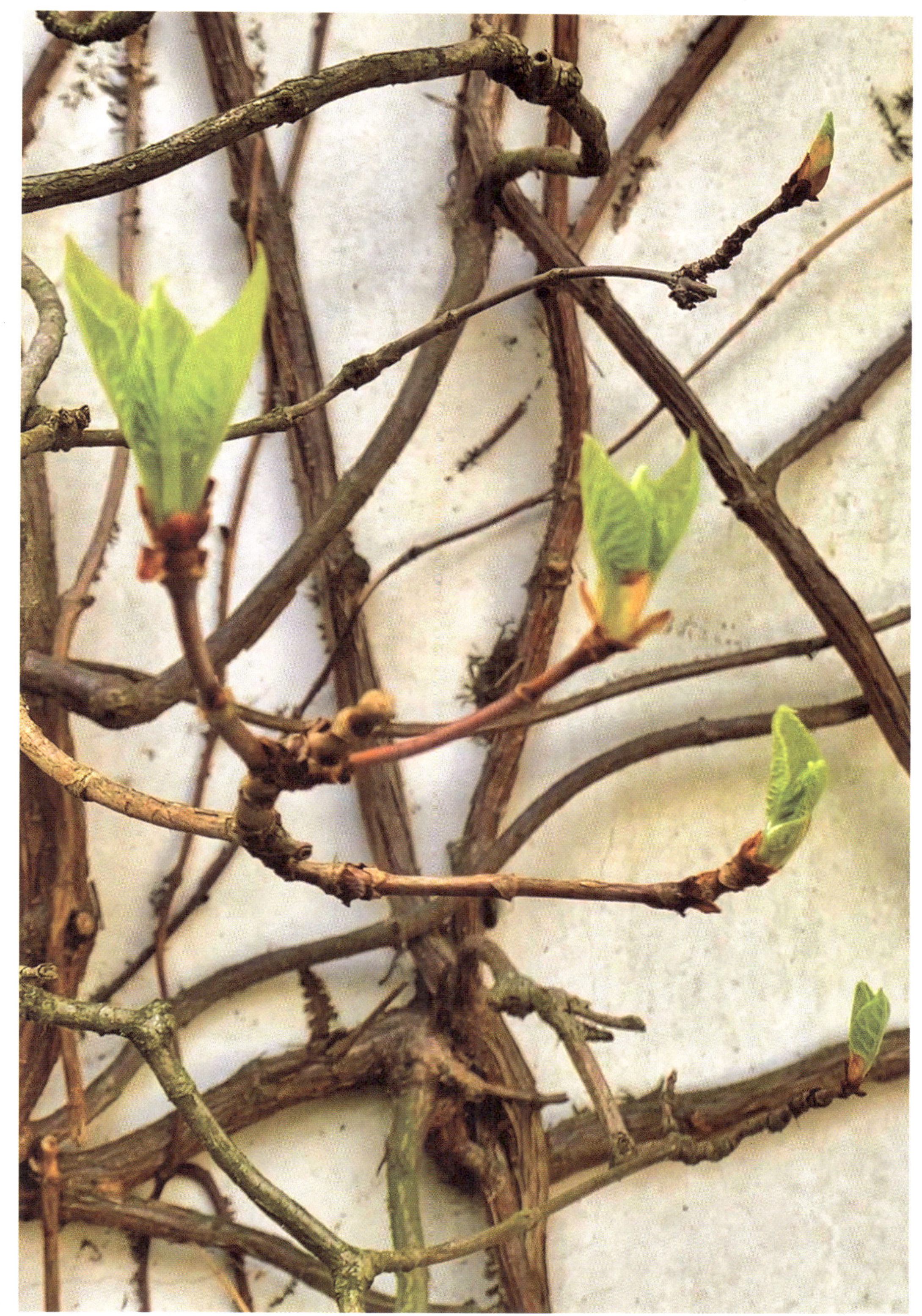

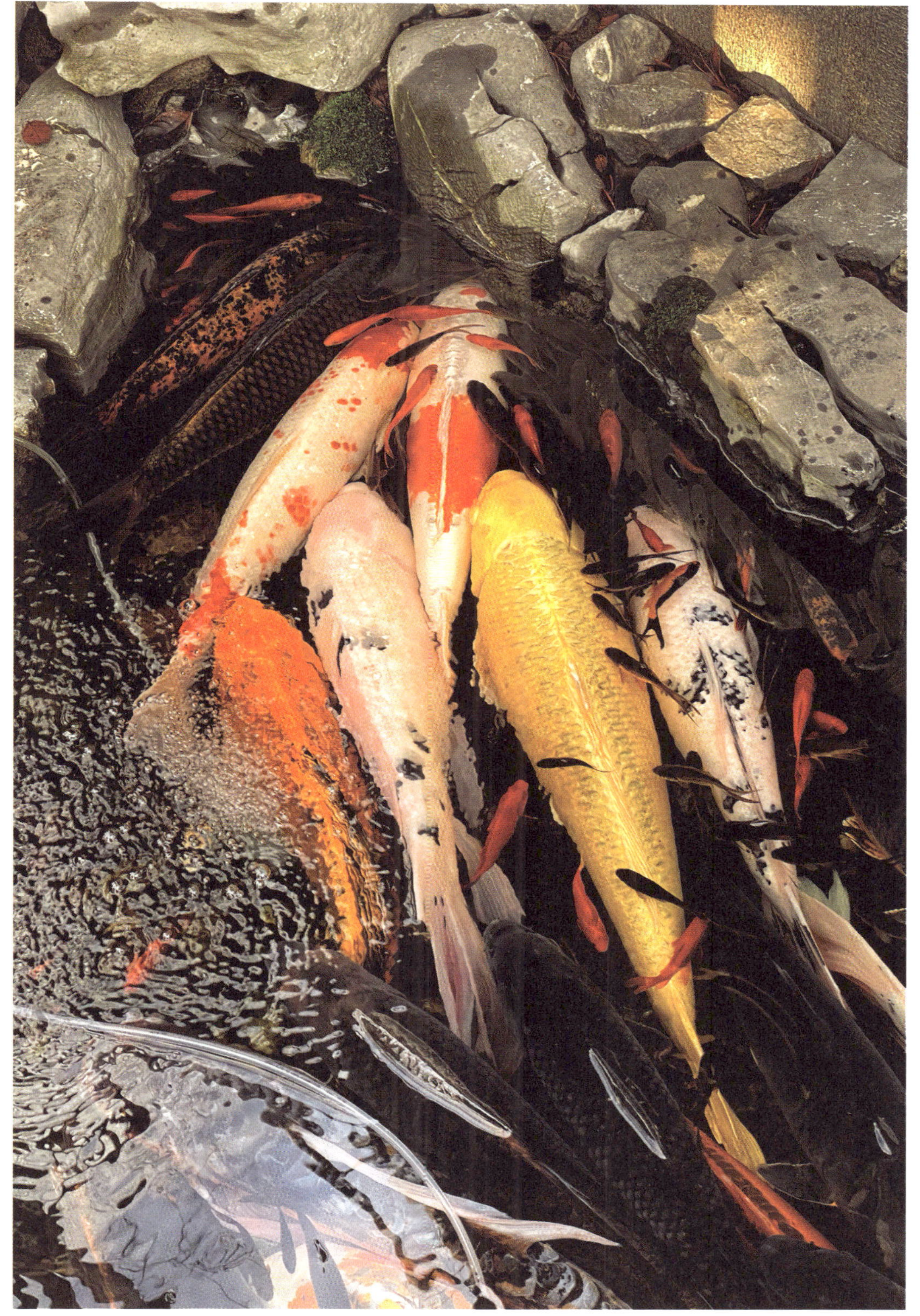

Hibernating

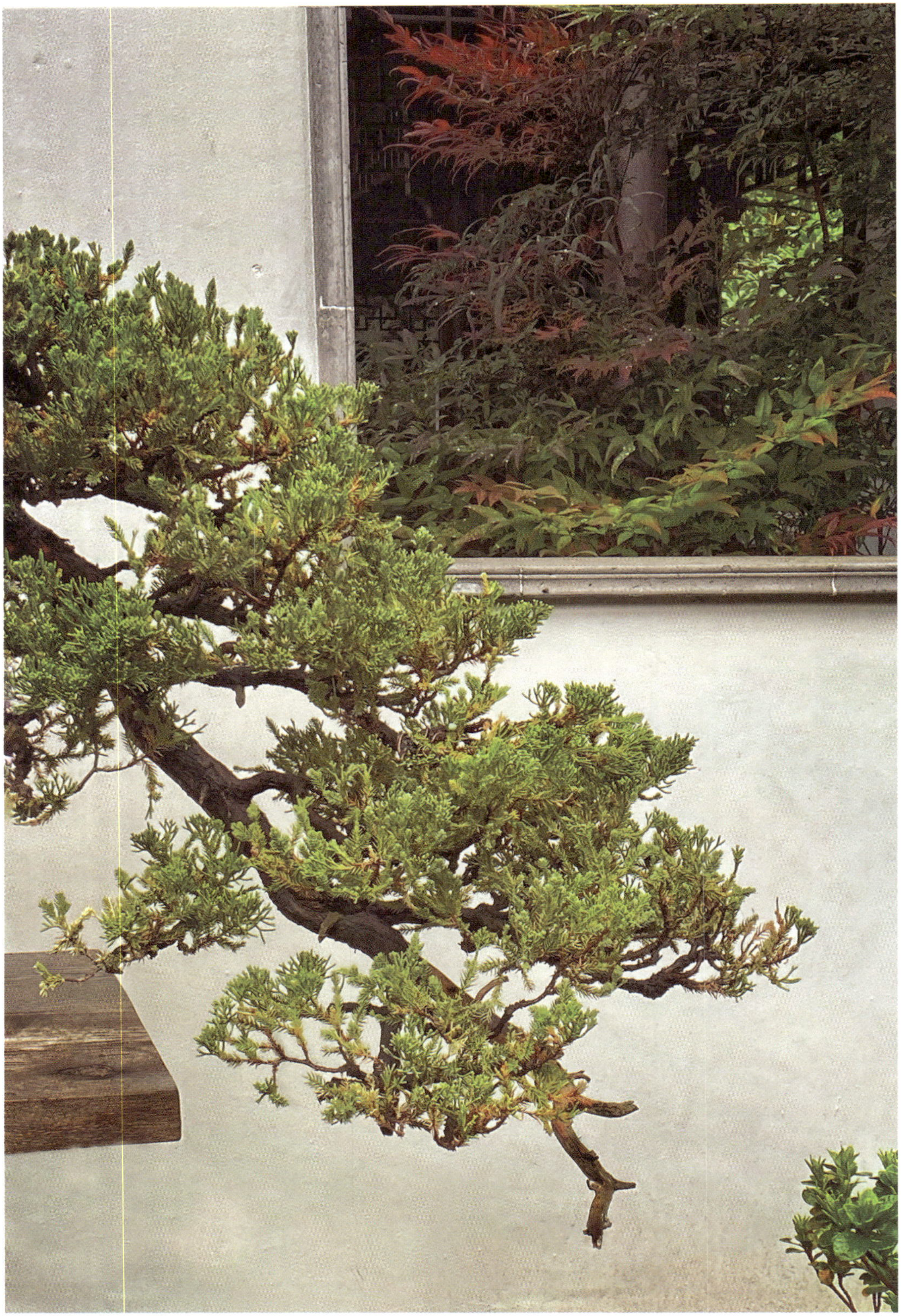

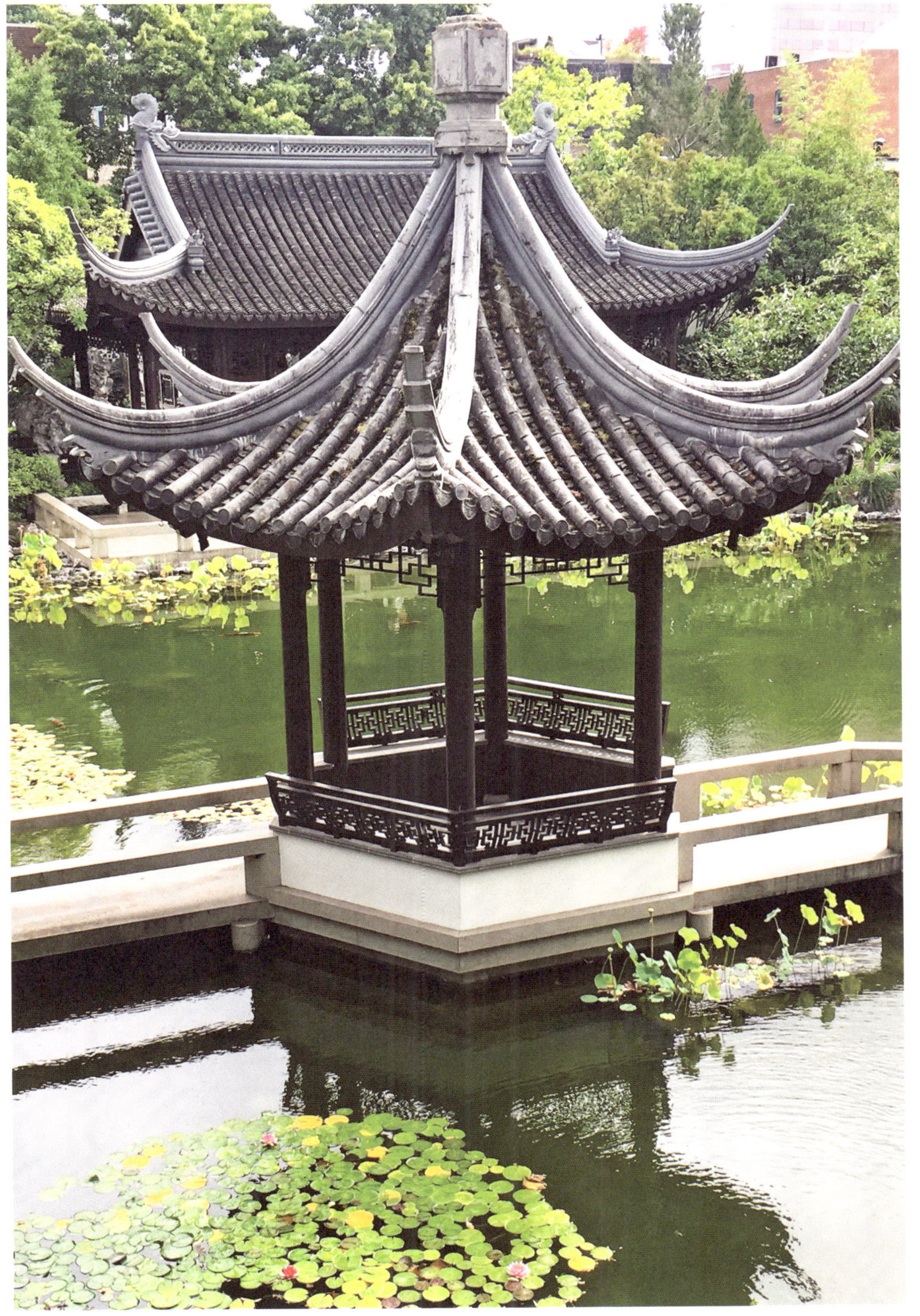

Ting Pagoda

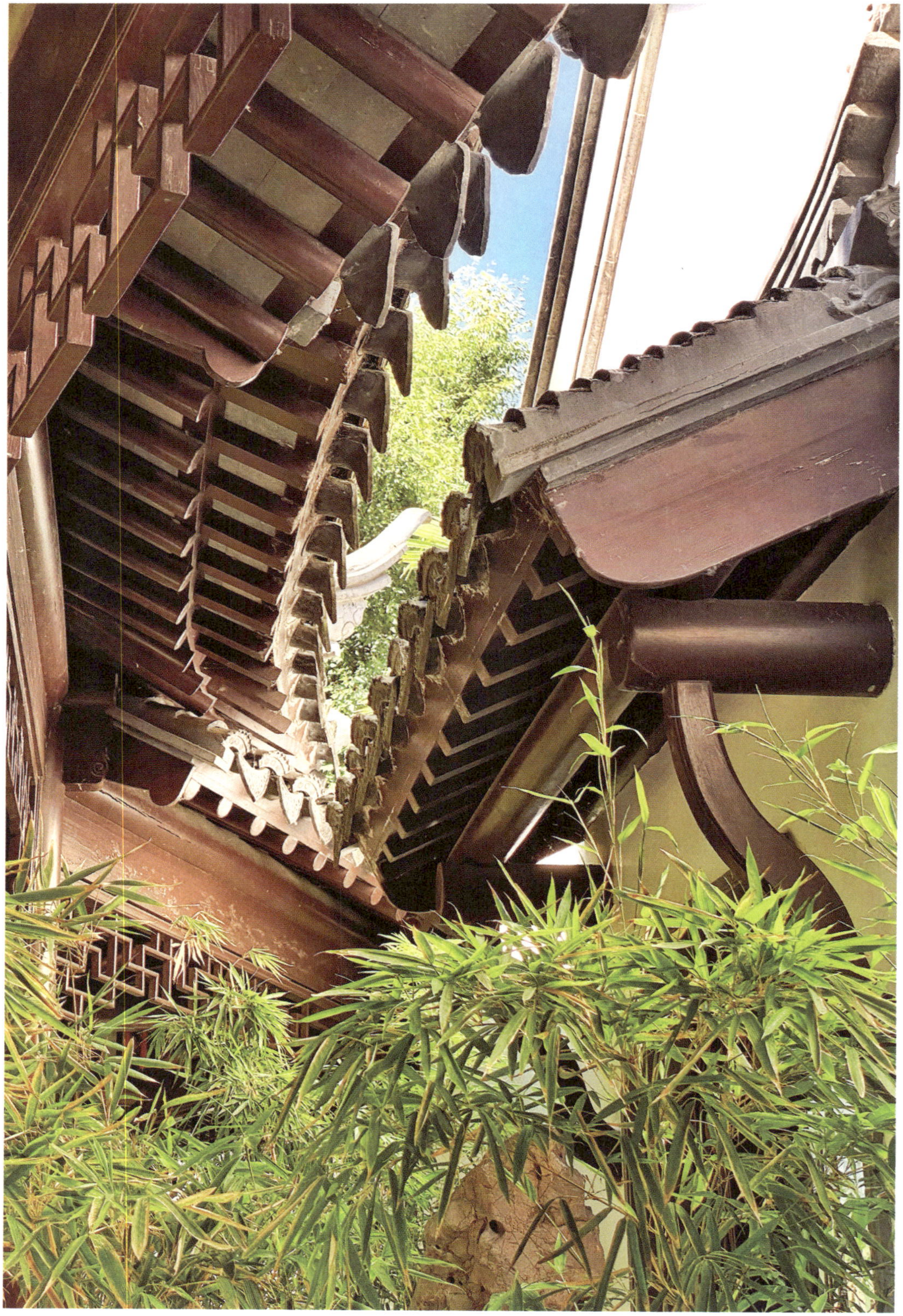

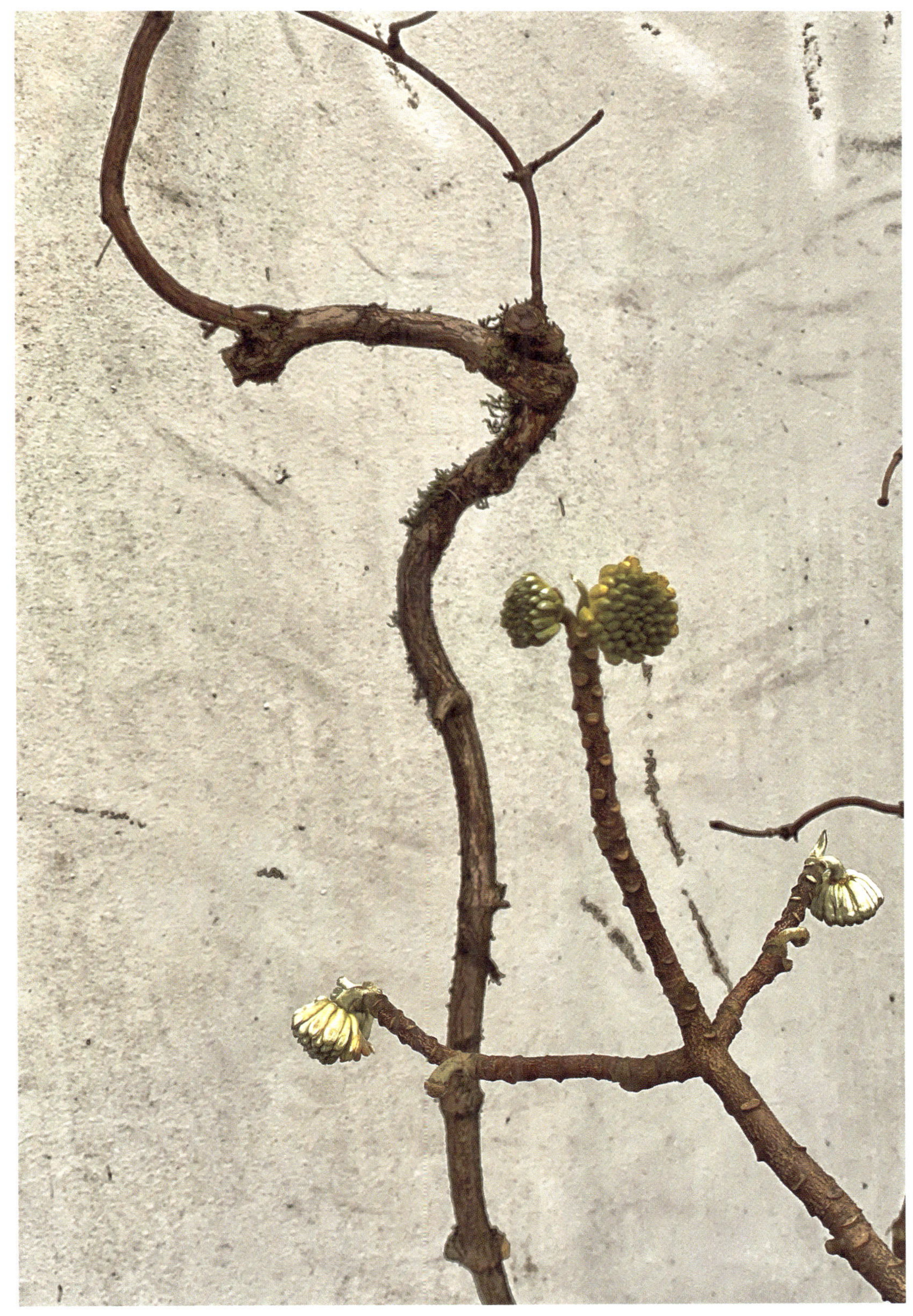

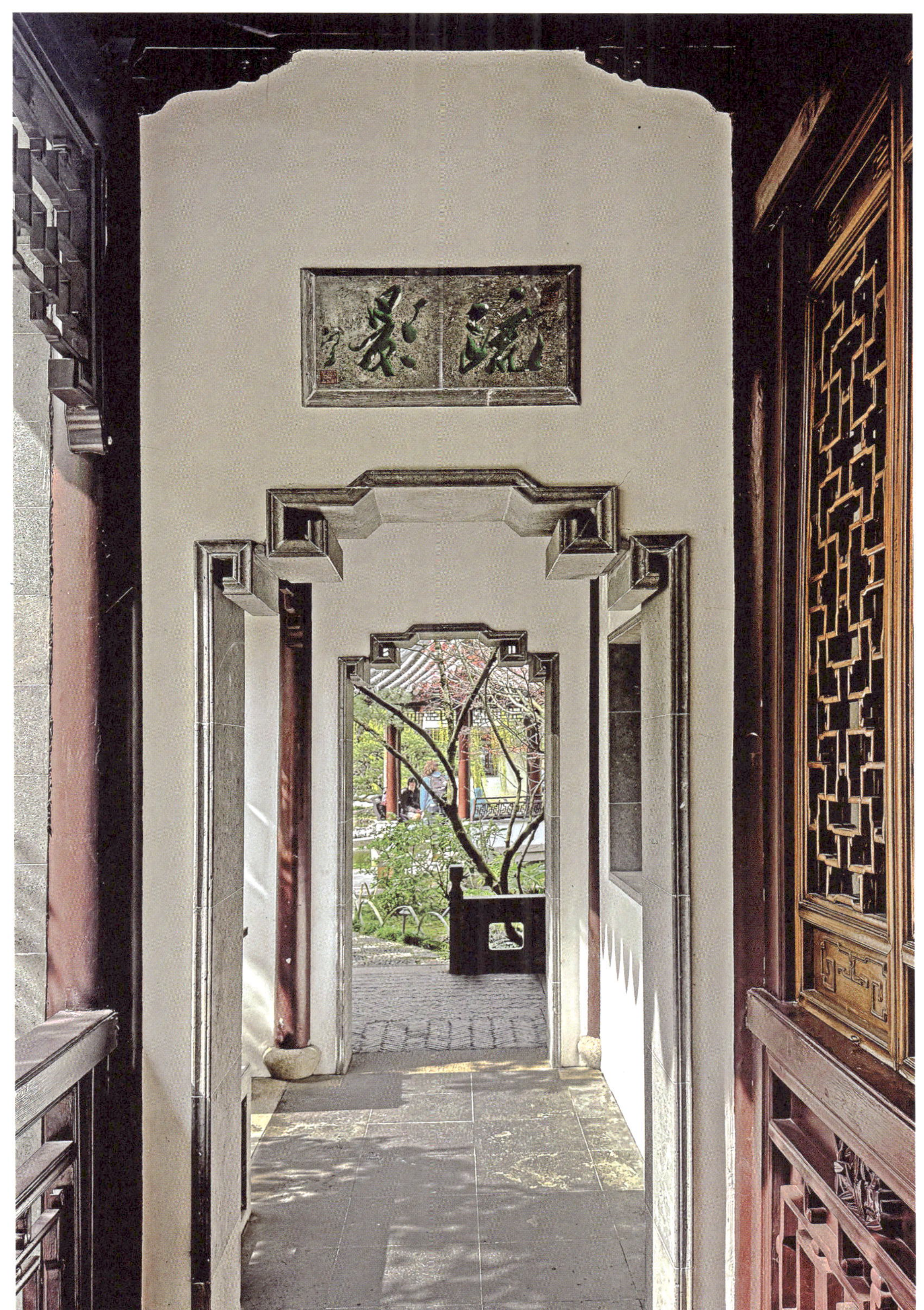

Inscription:
Scattered Shadows
shu ying

29

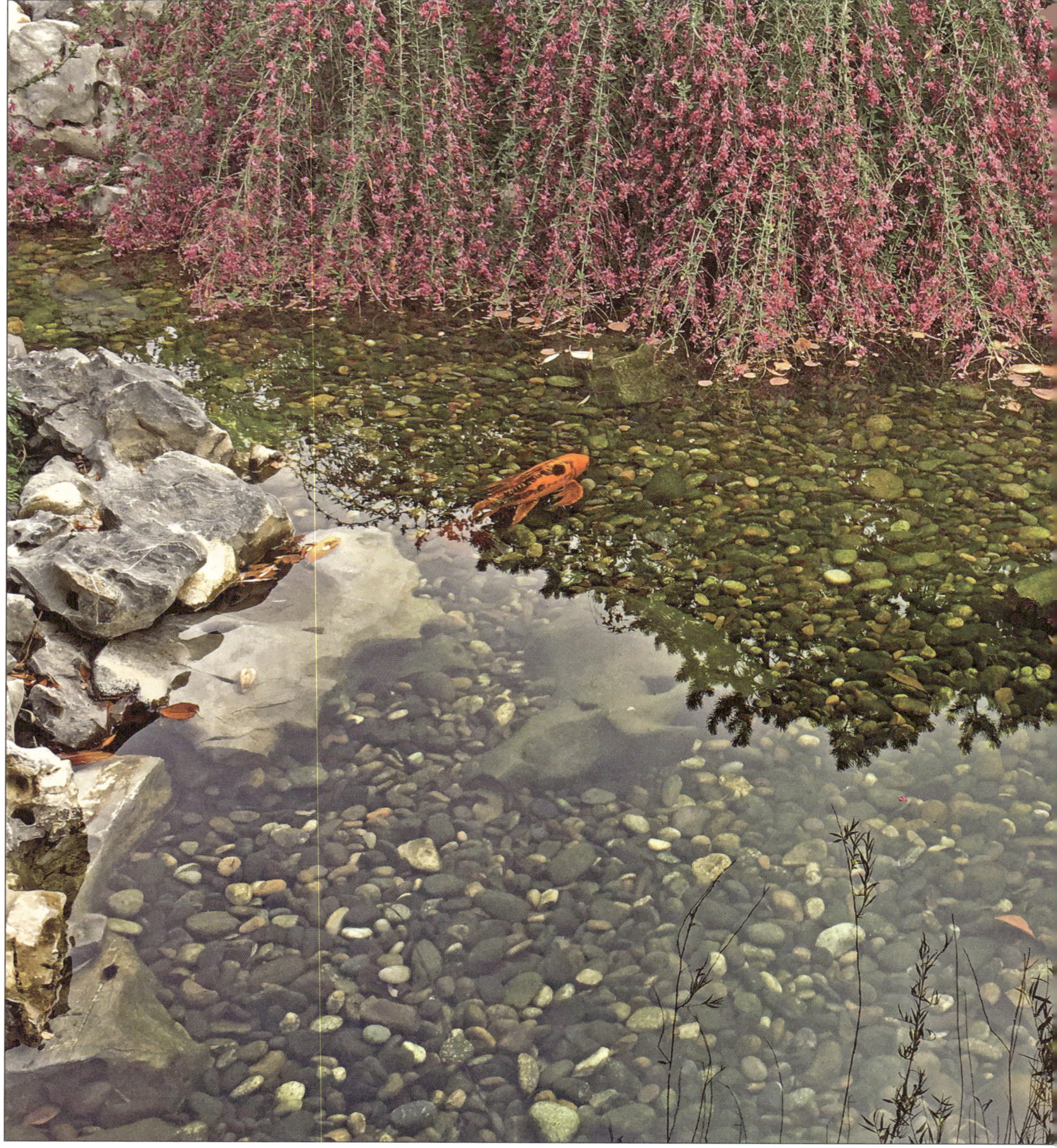

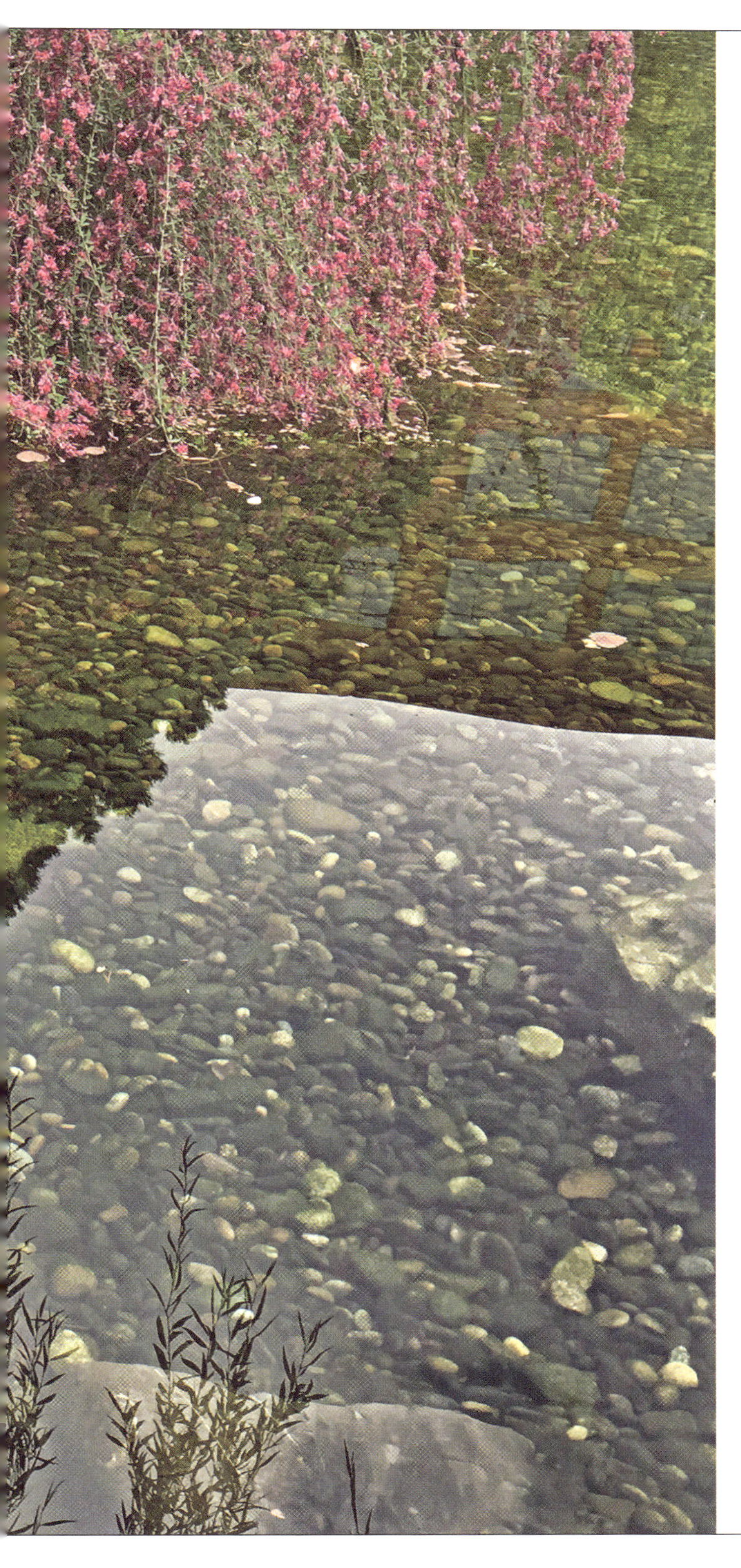

WELCOME
SPRING

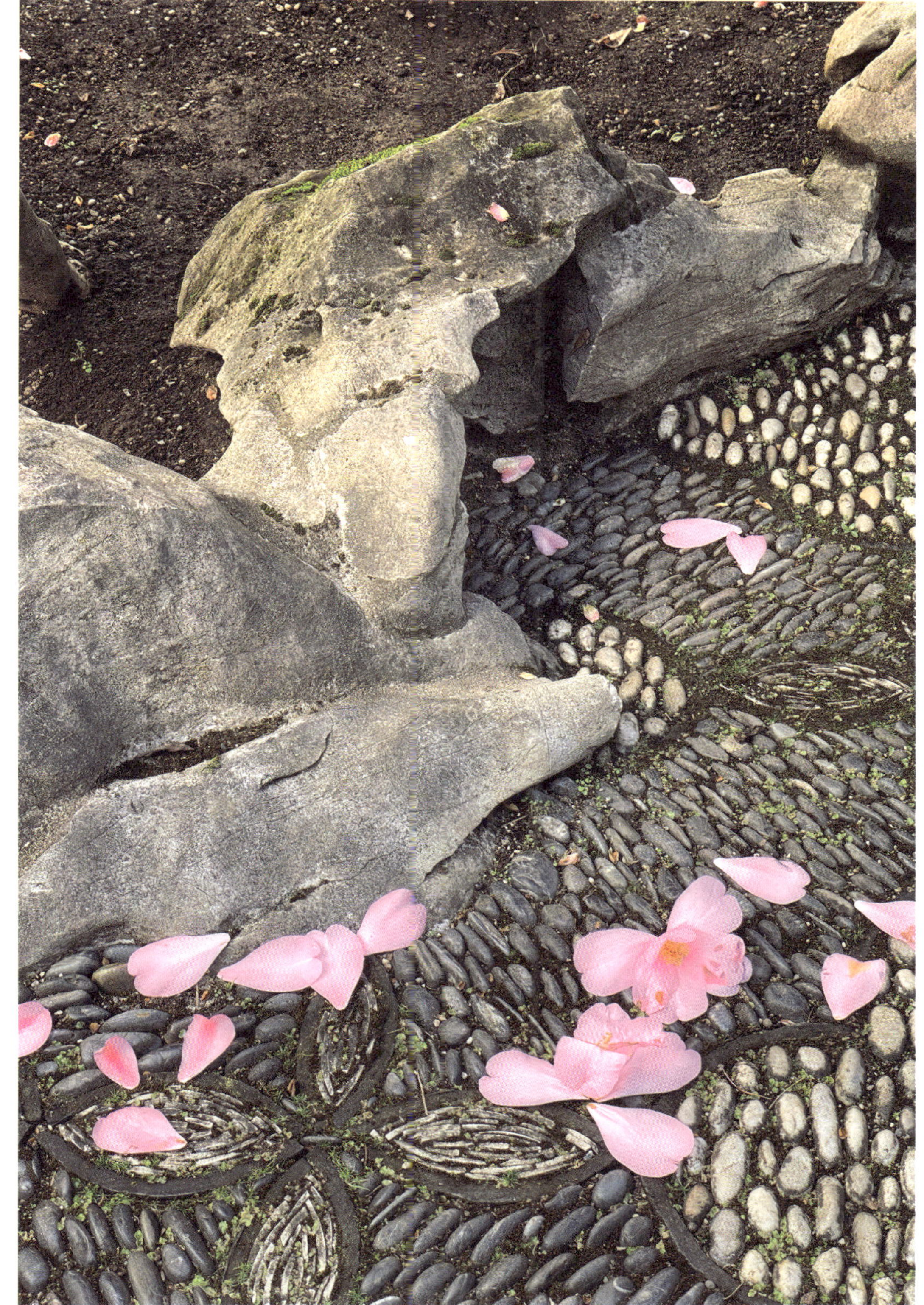

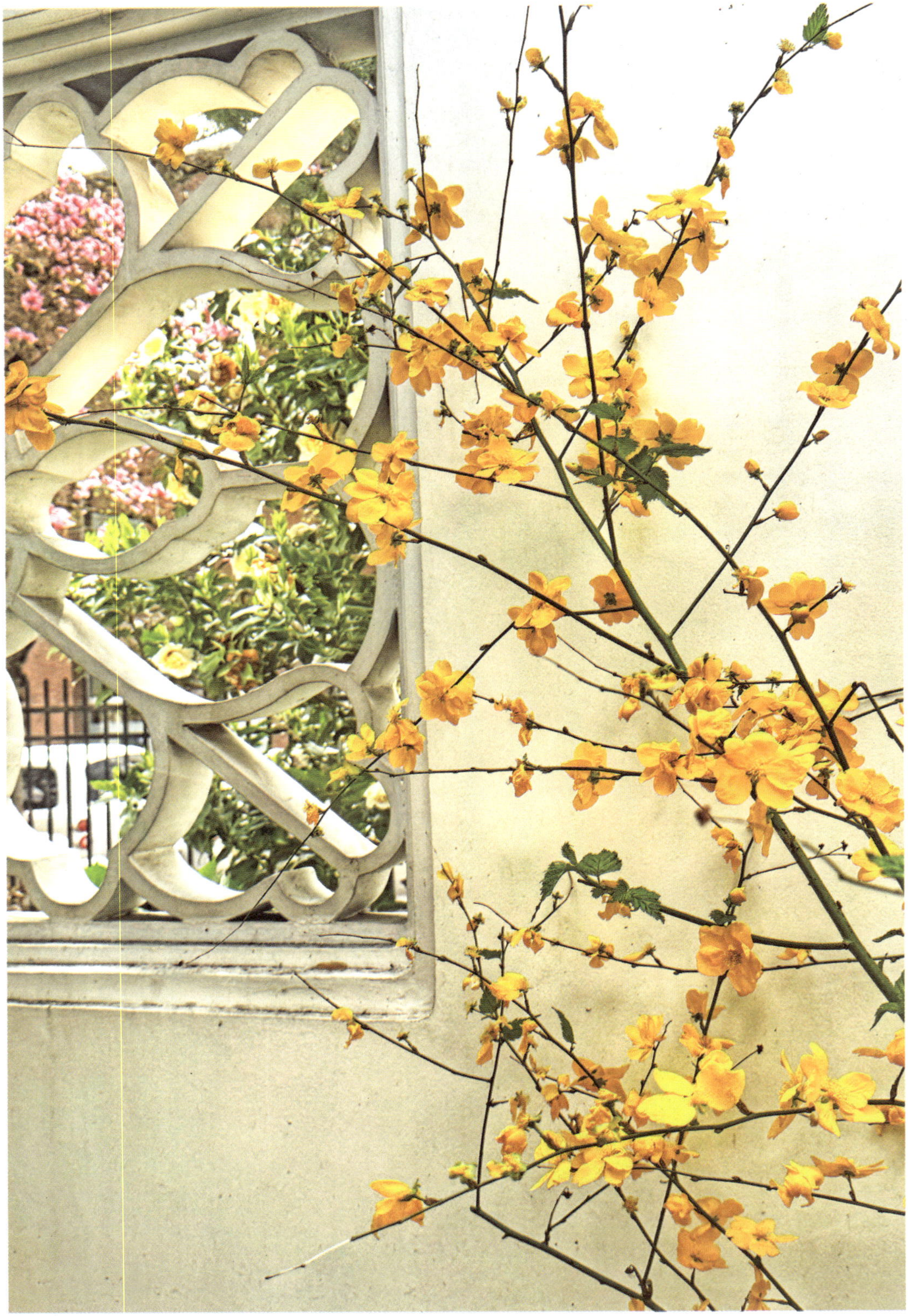

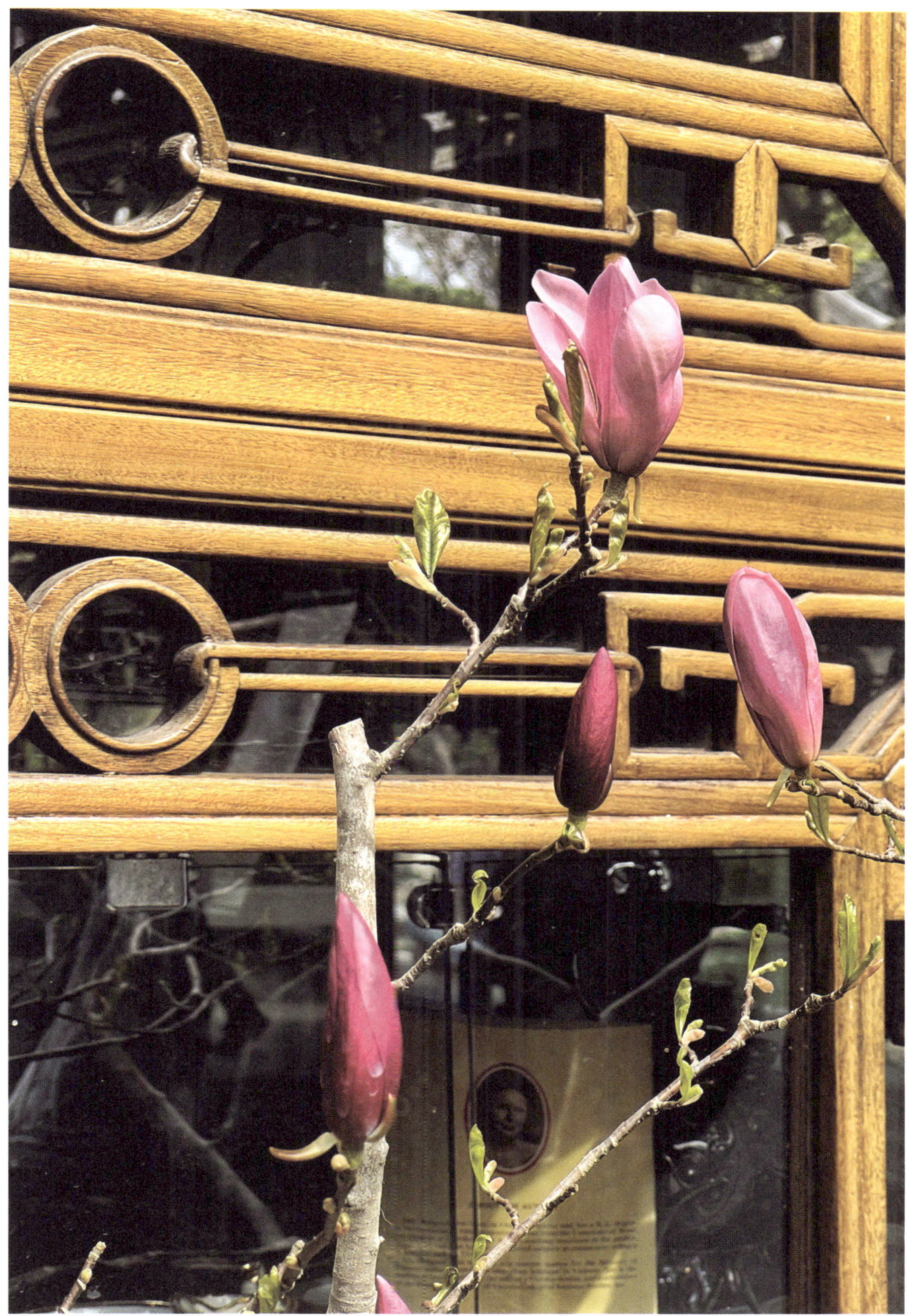

Pink Magnolia Buds

Purple Lily Pads

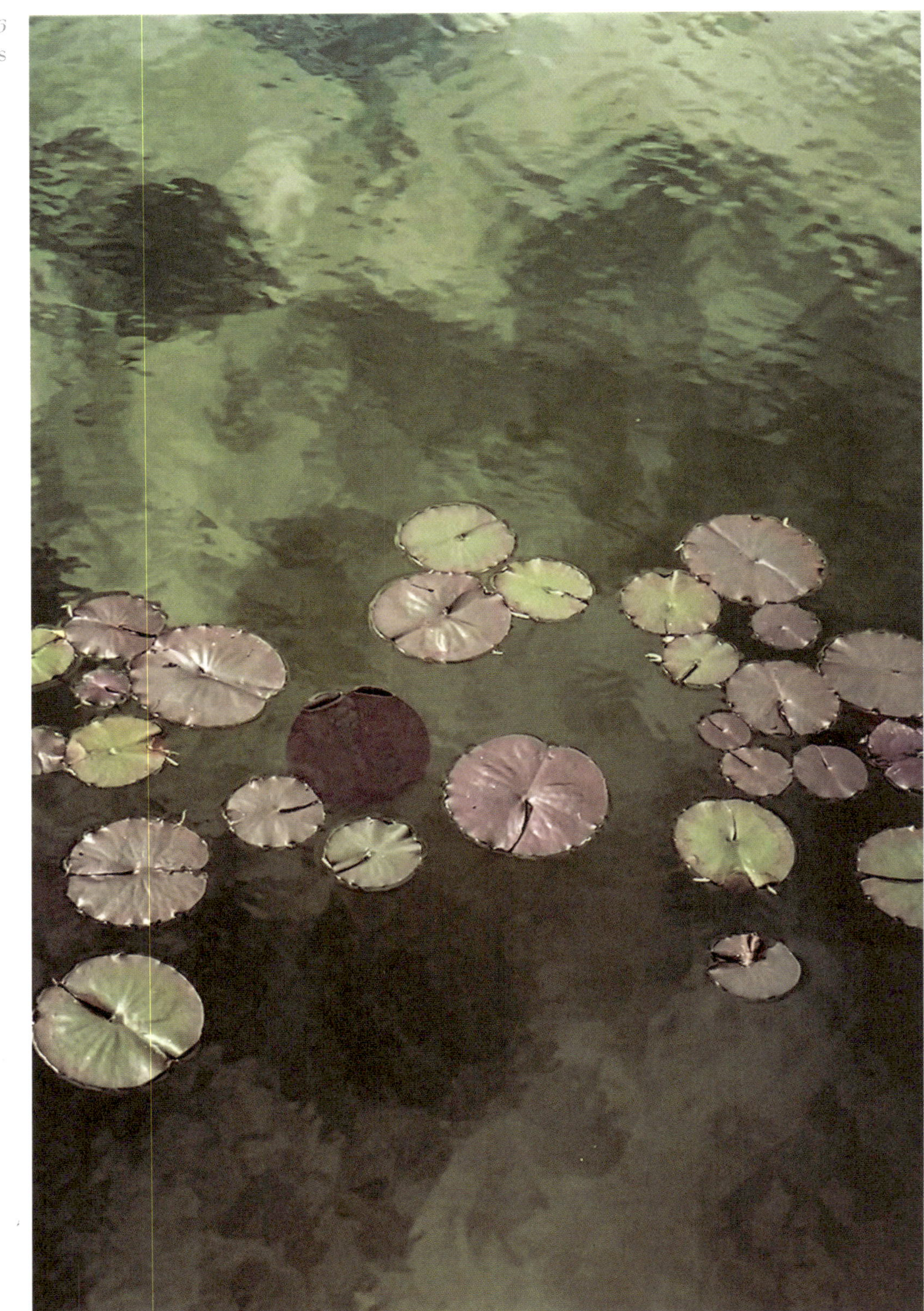

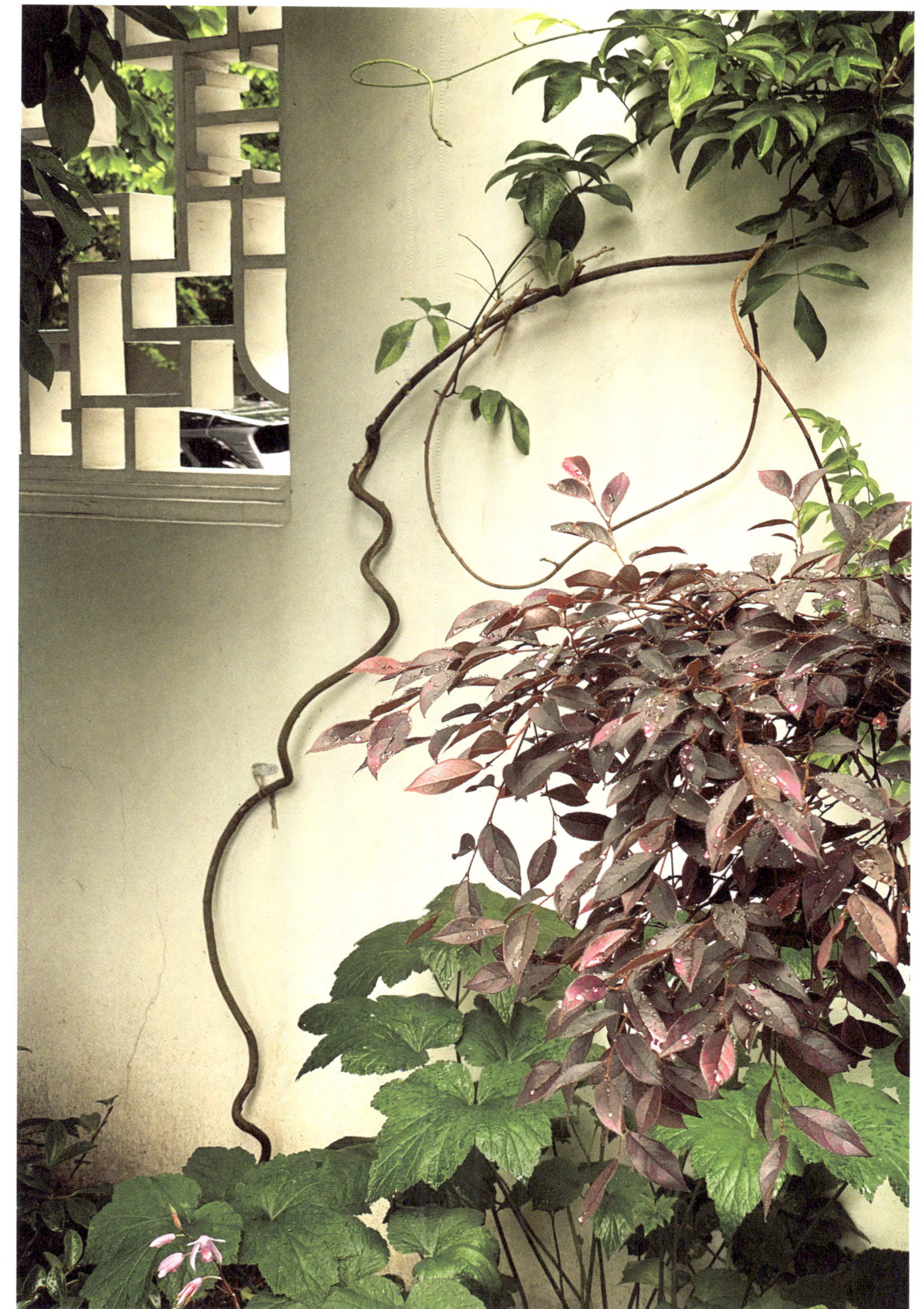

Line Drawing
with "Leak Windows"

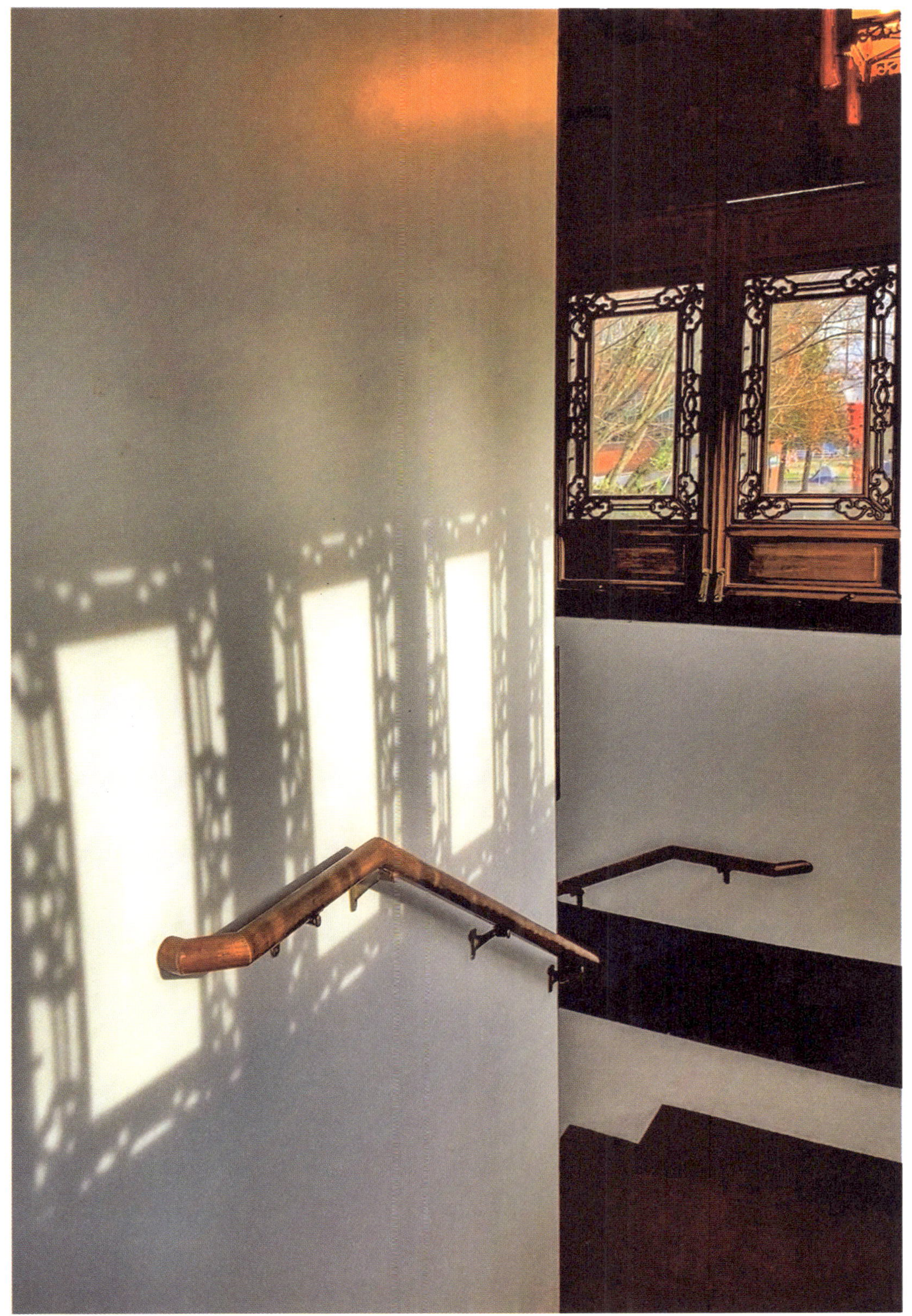

Window Shadows

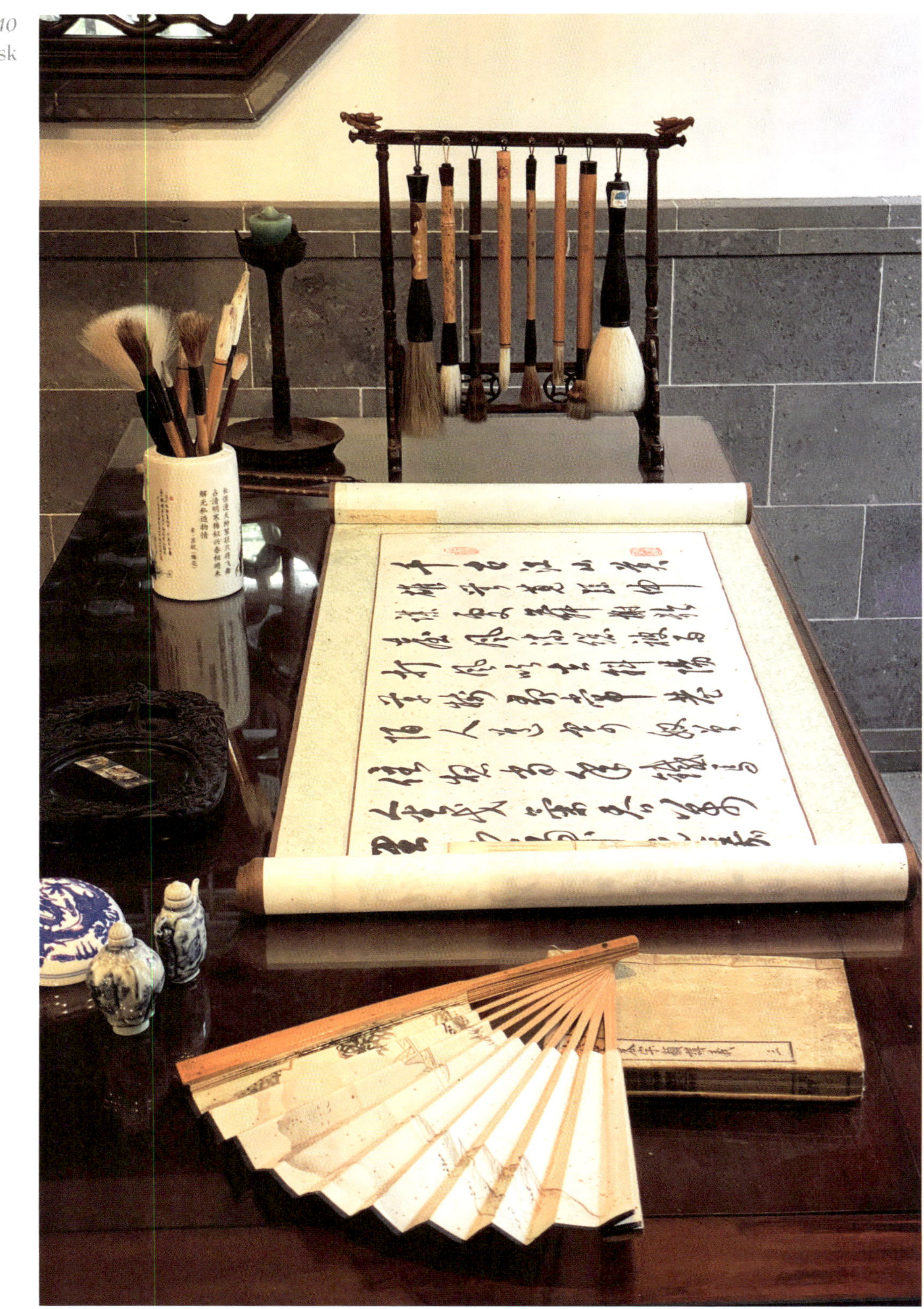

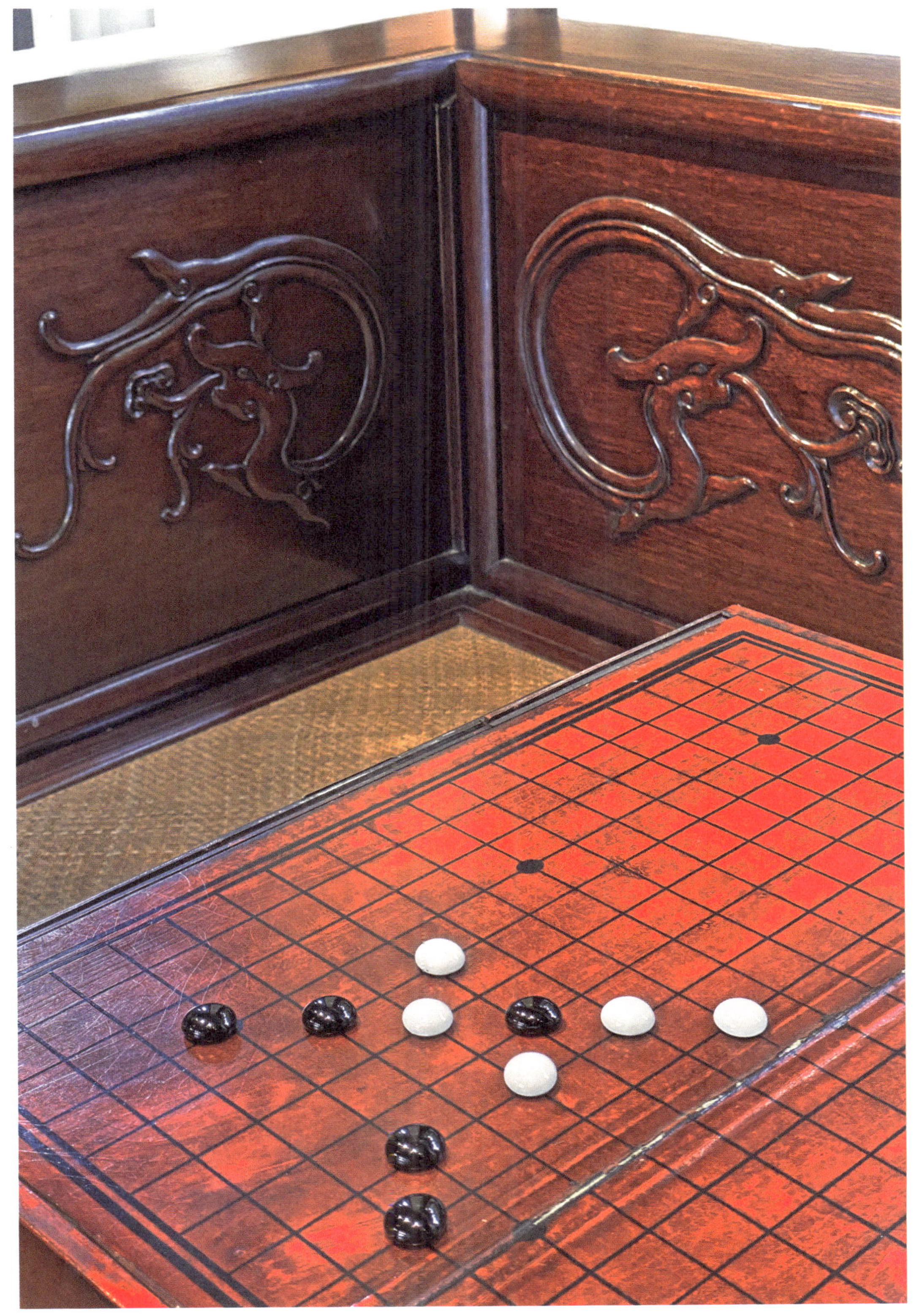

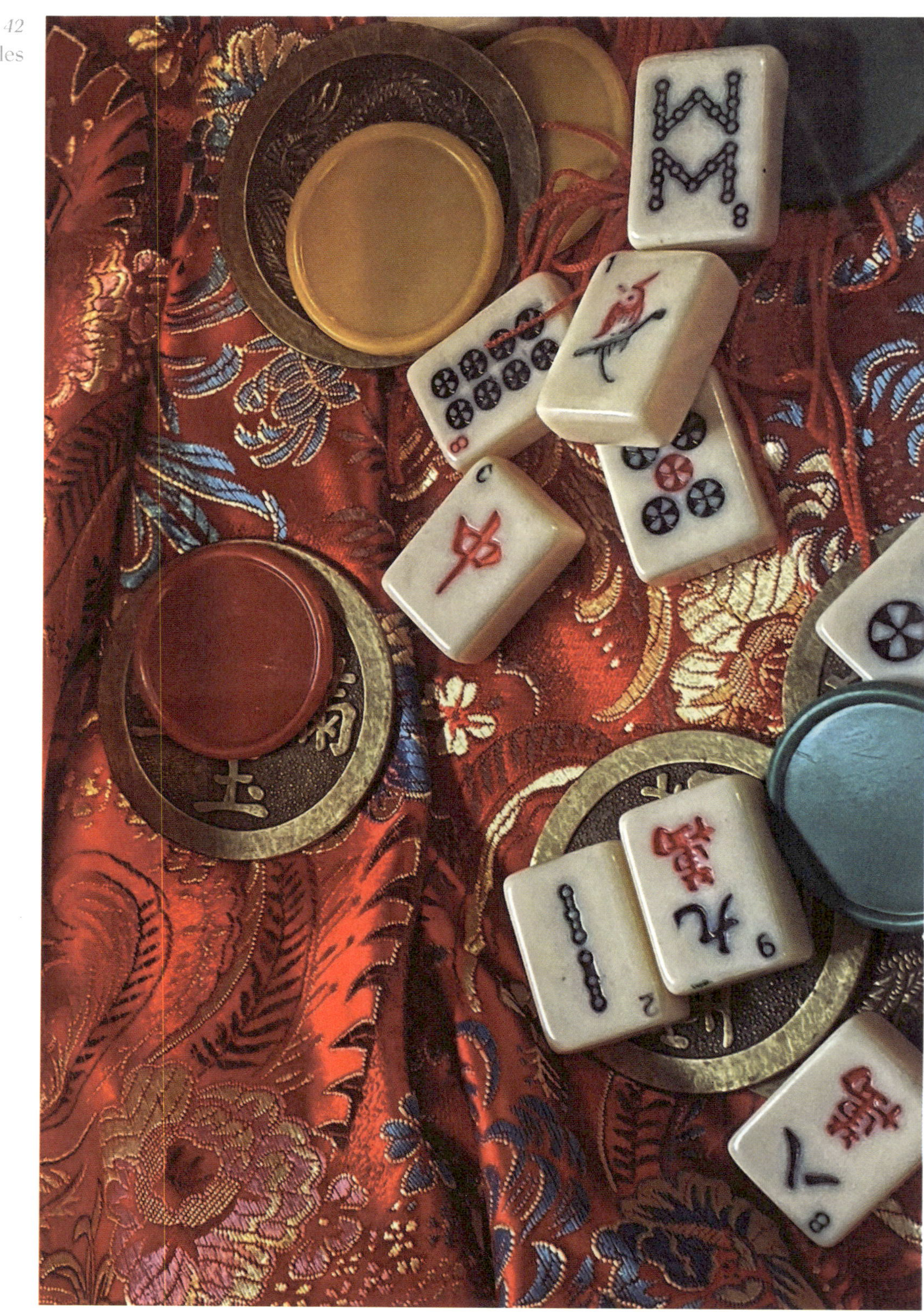

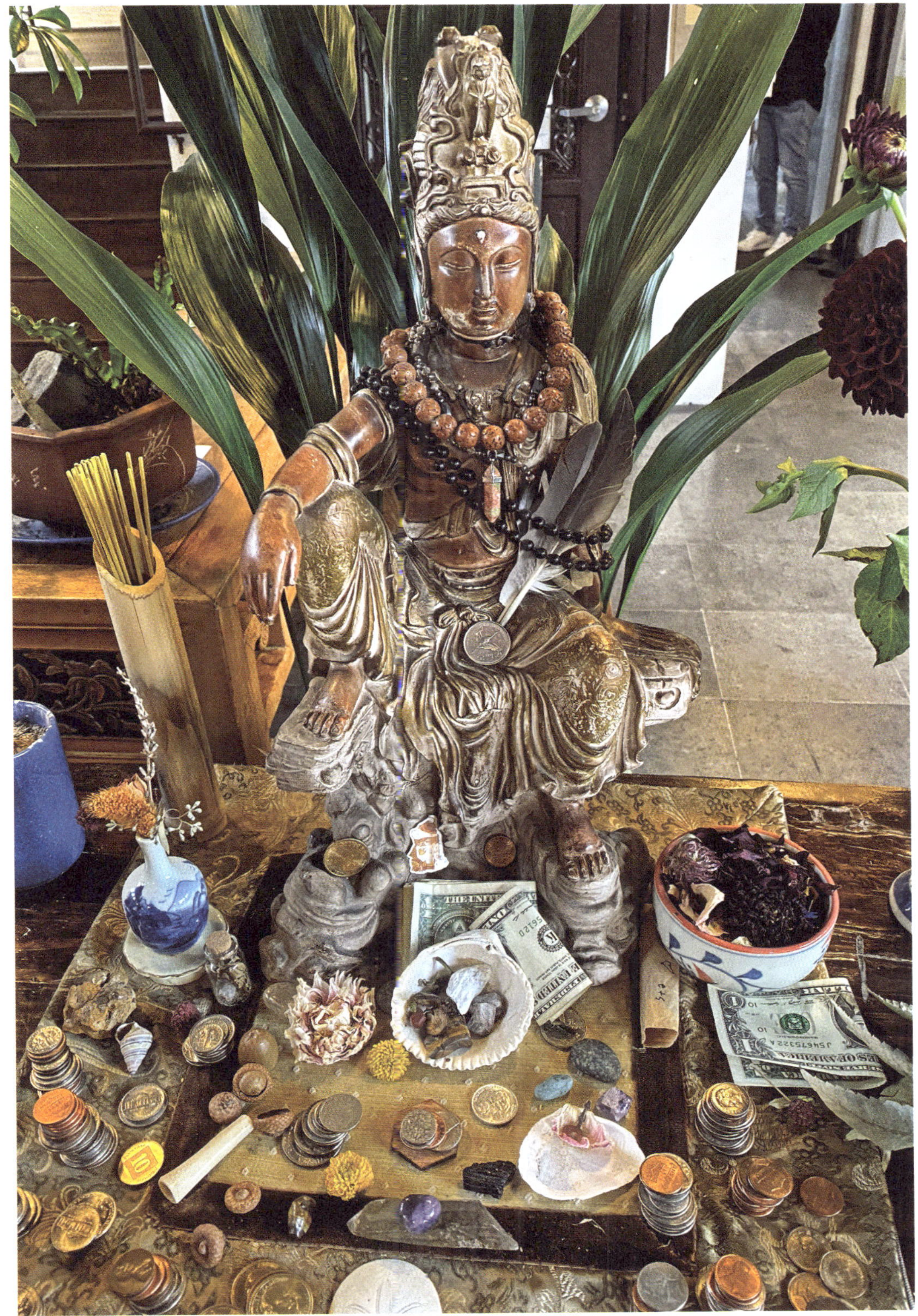

Guan Yin

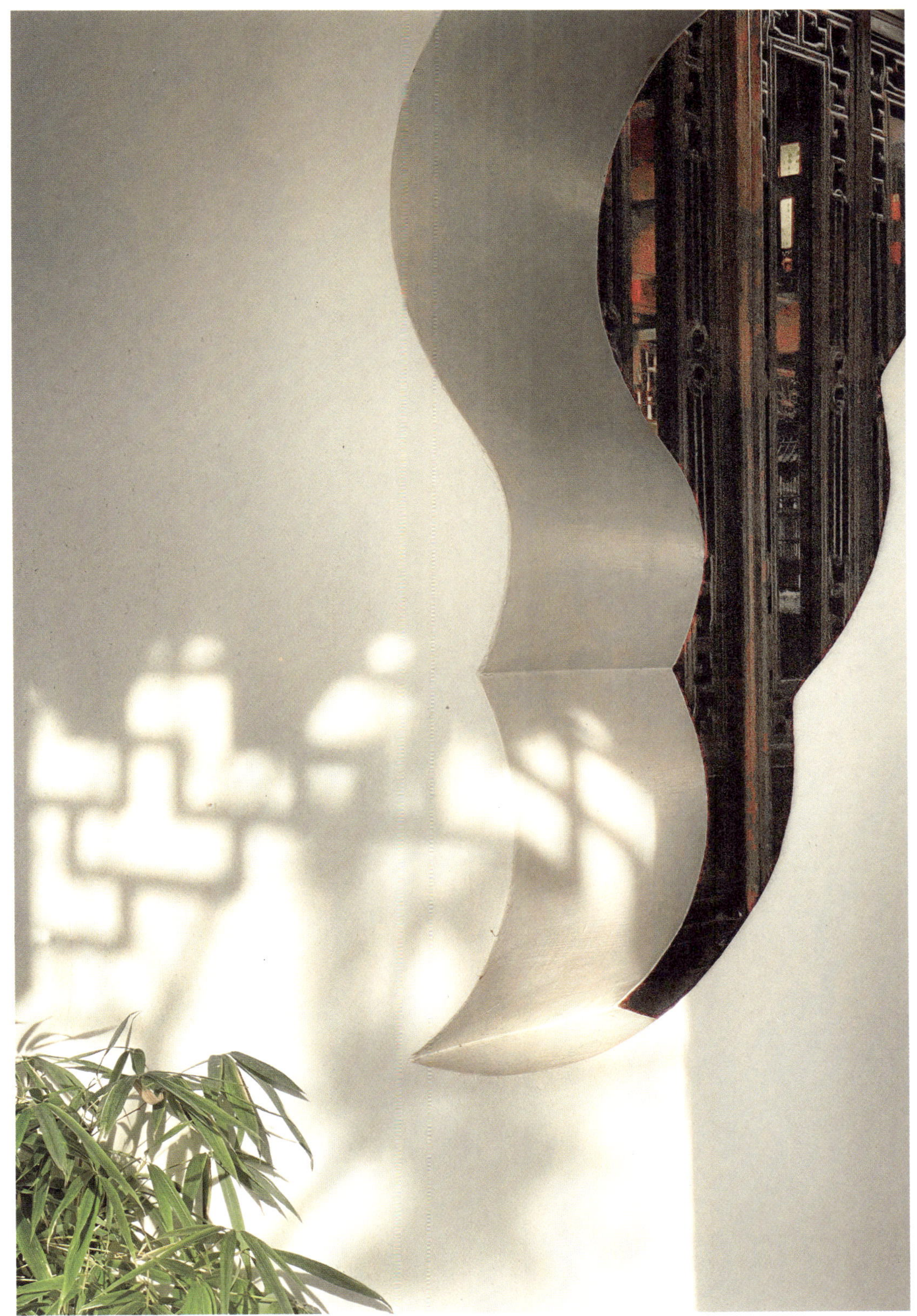

Pepper Window with
Good Luck Shadows

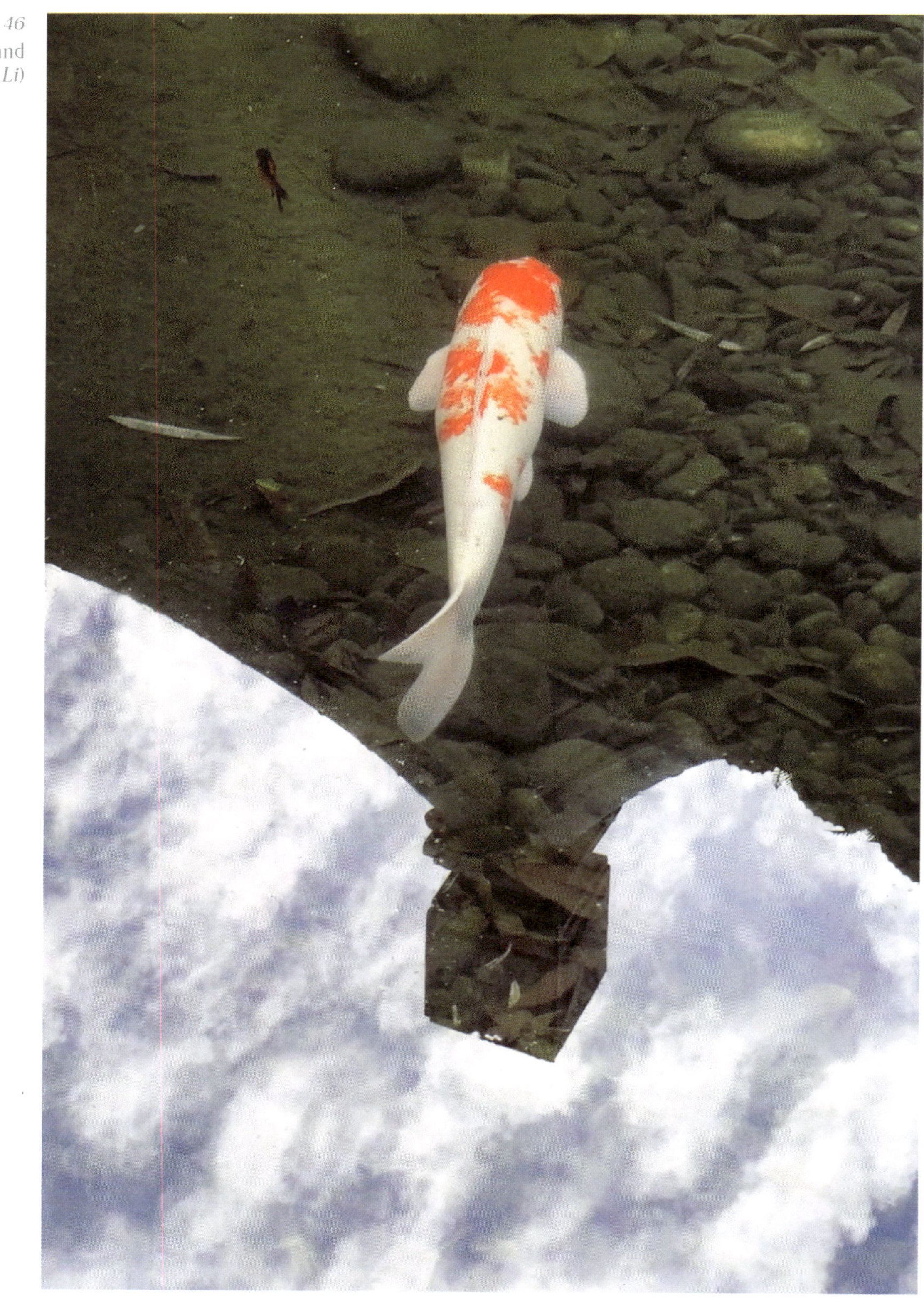

46
Sky, Stones, and
Koi (*Jin Li*)

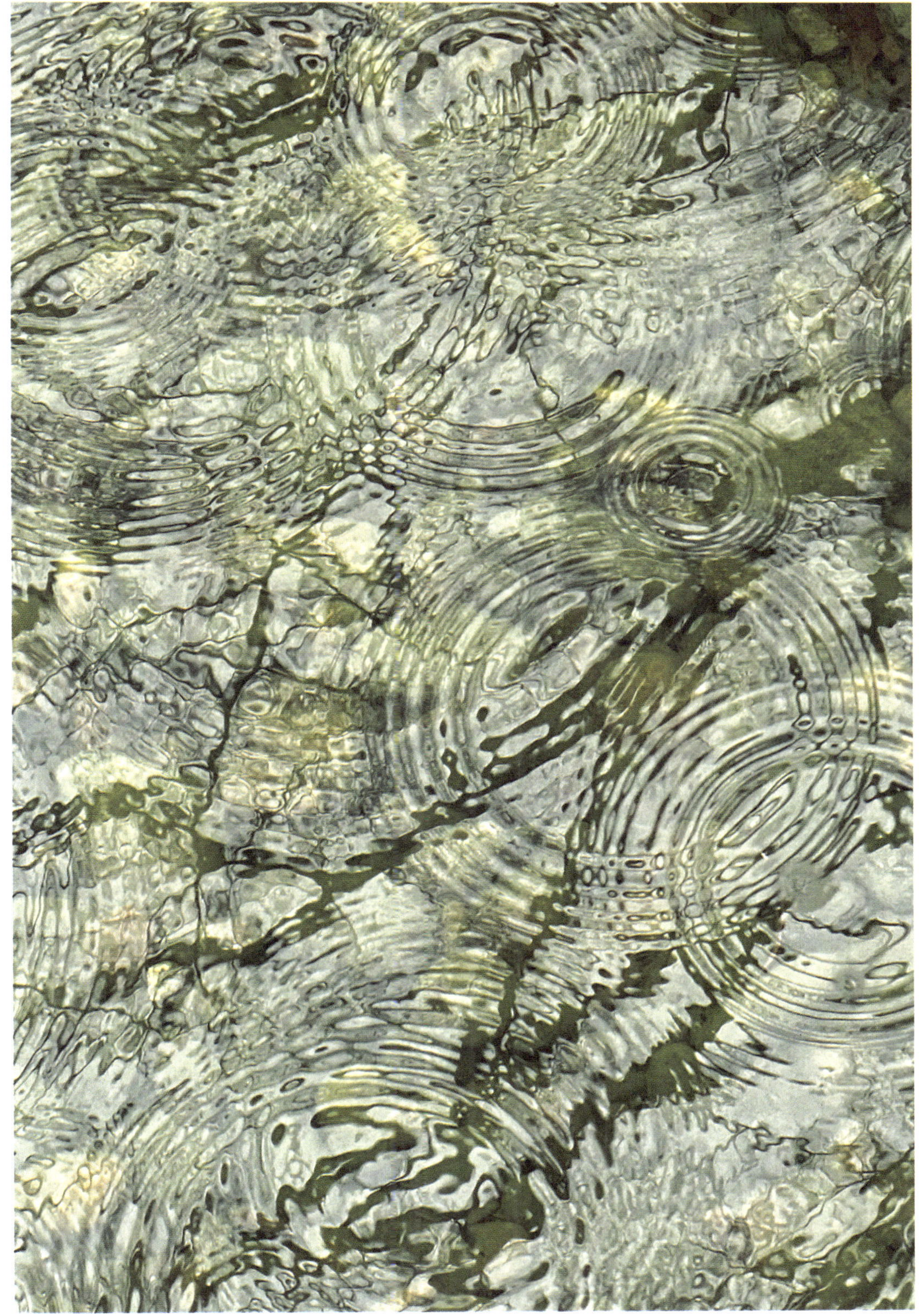

Rain

47

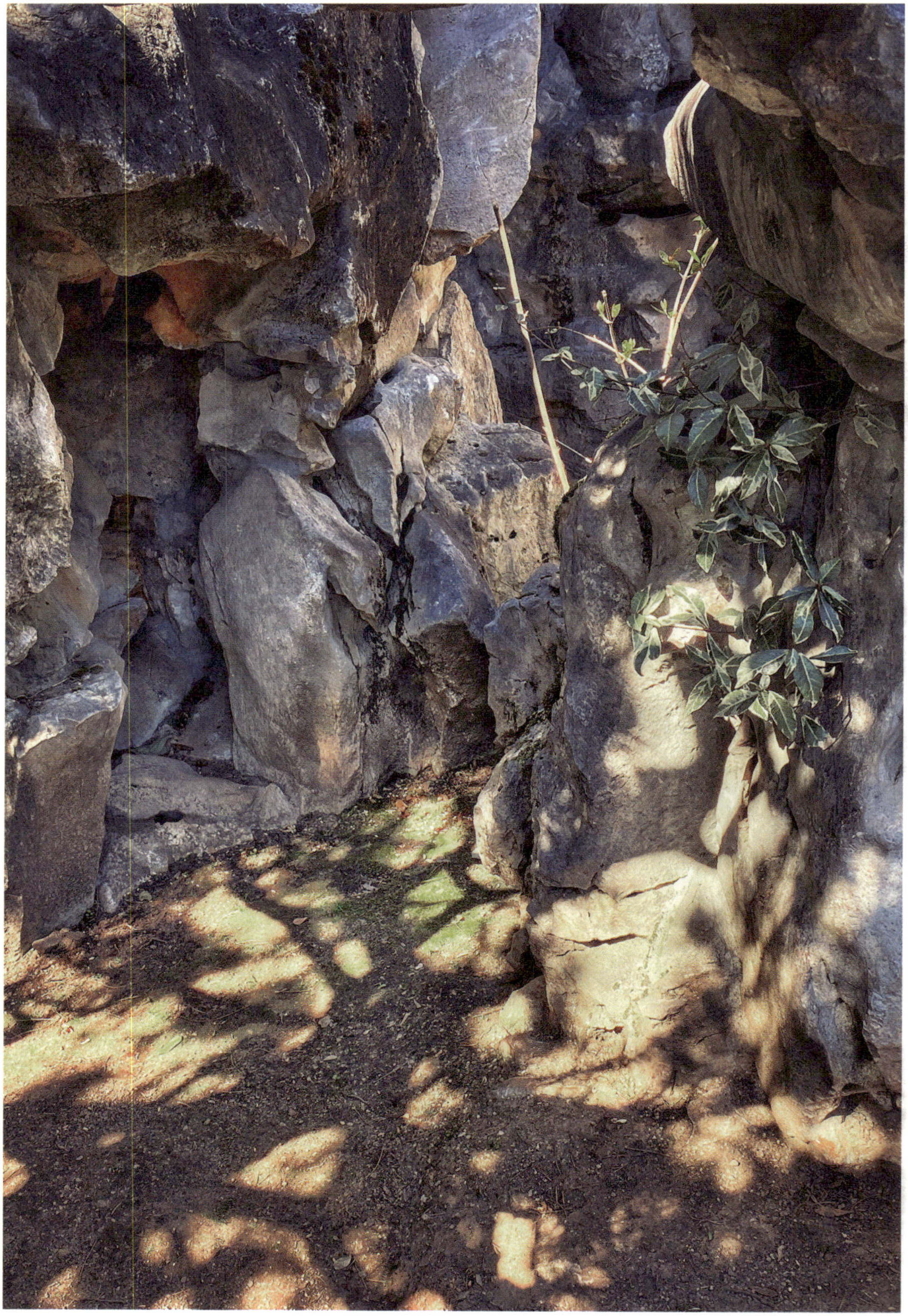

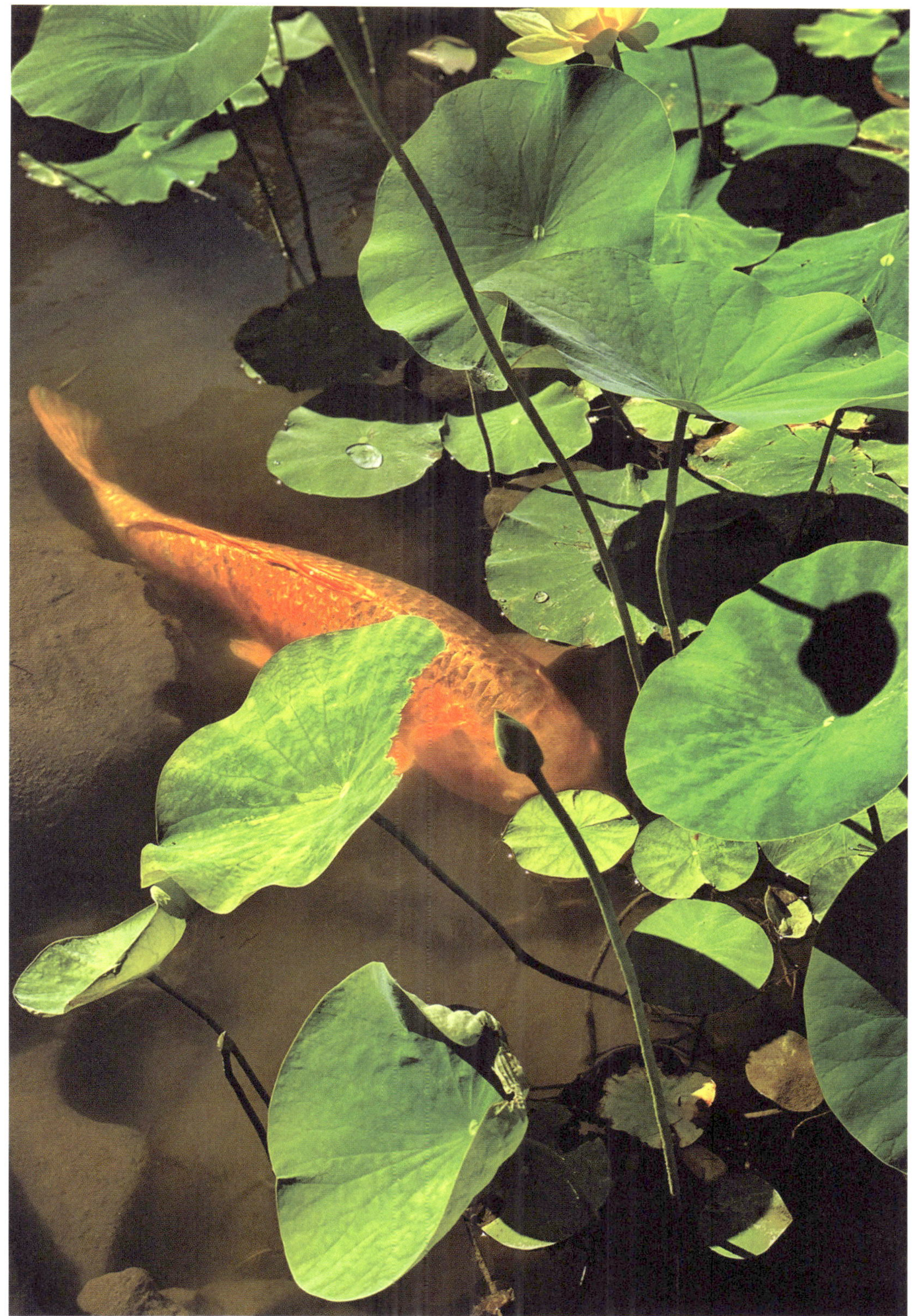

Hiding Koi
51

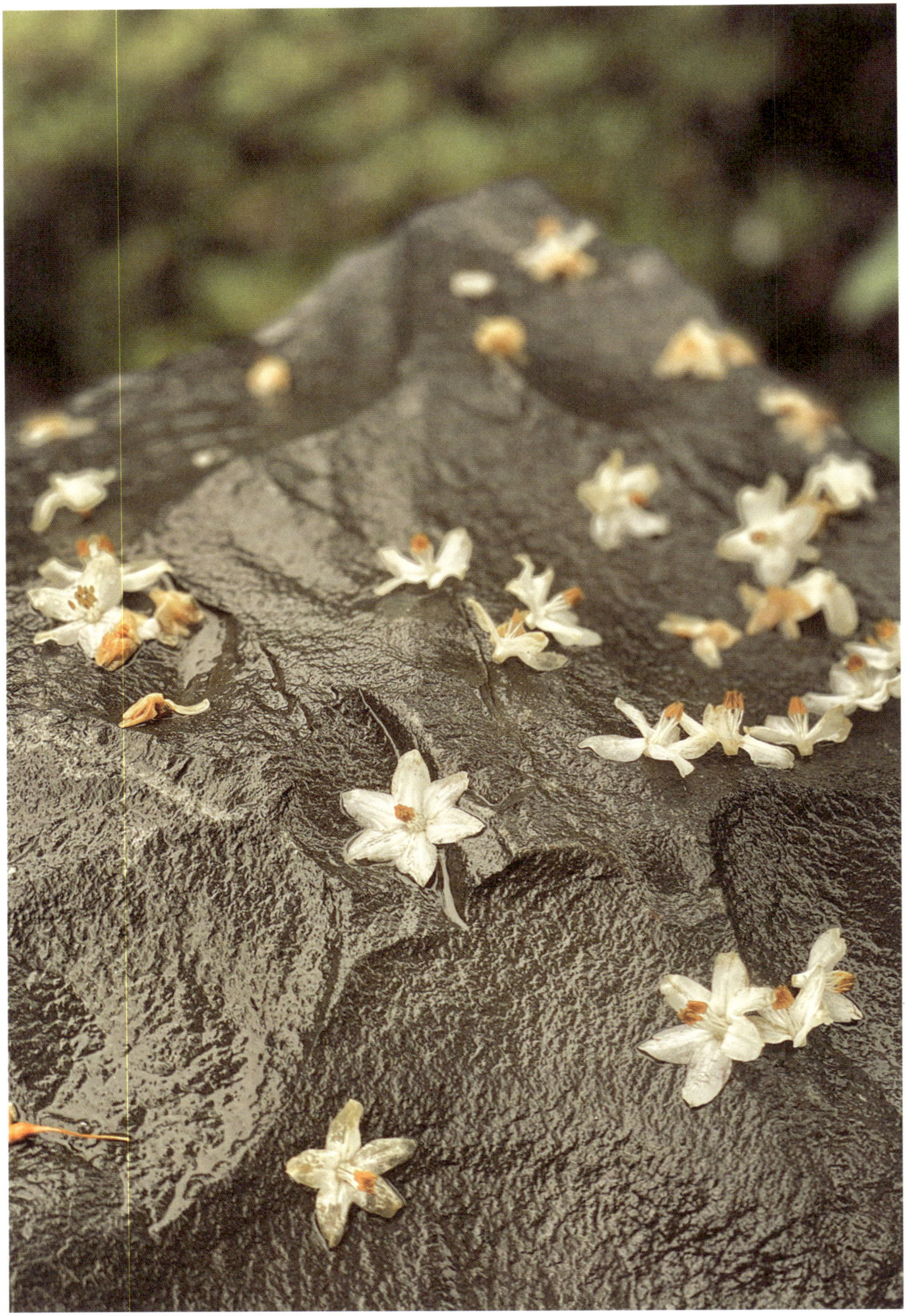

Stone and Flower
Details

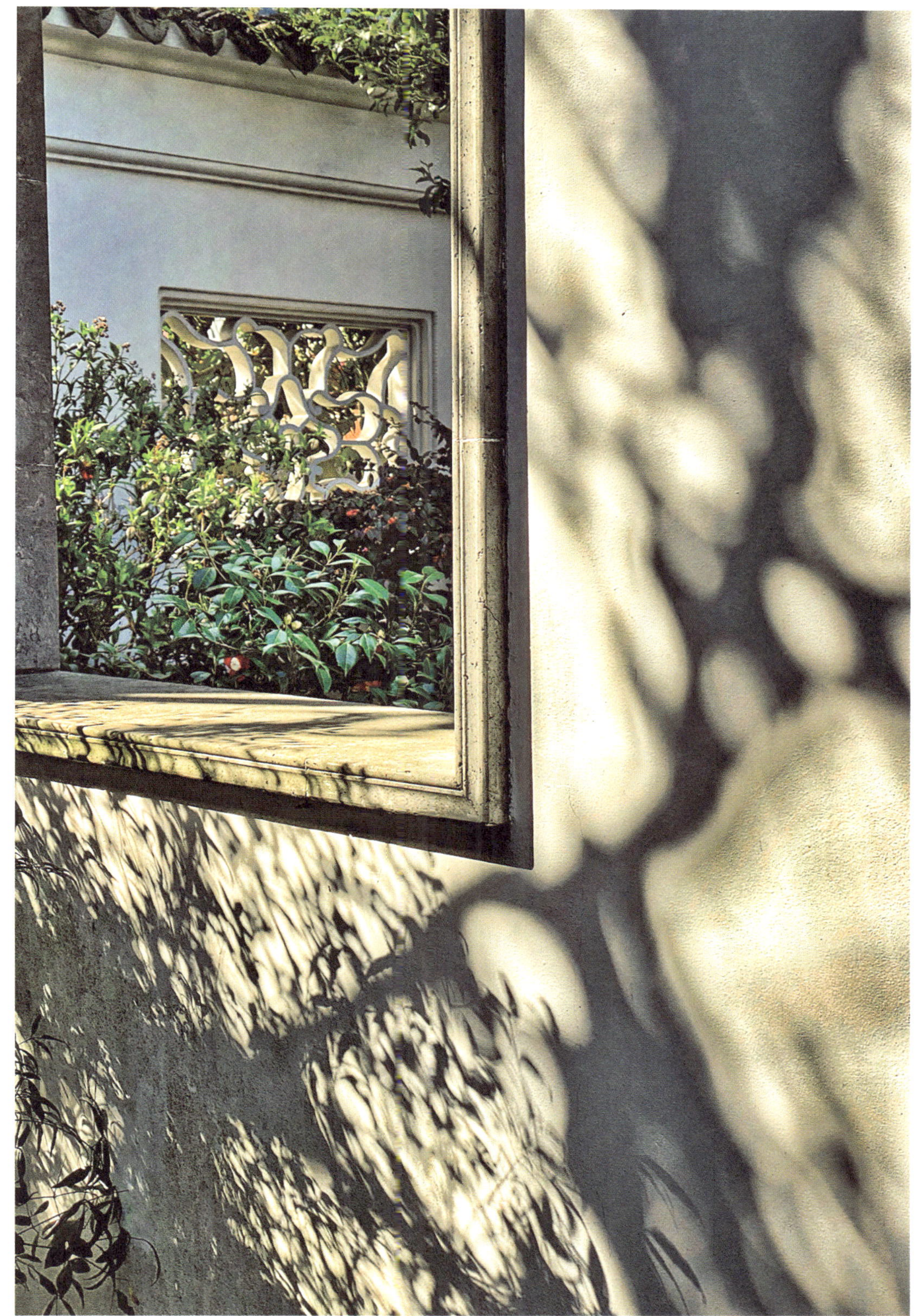

Window and Shadow

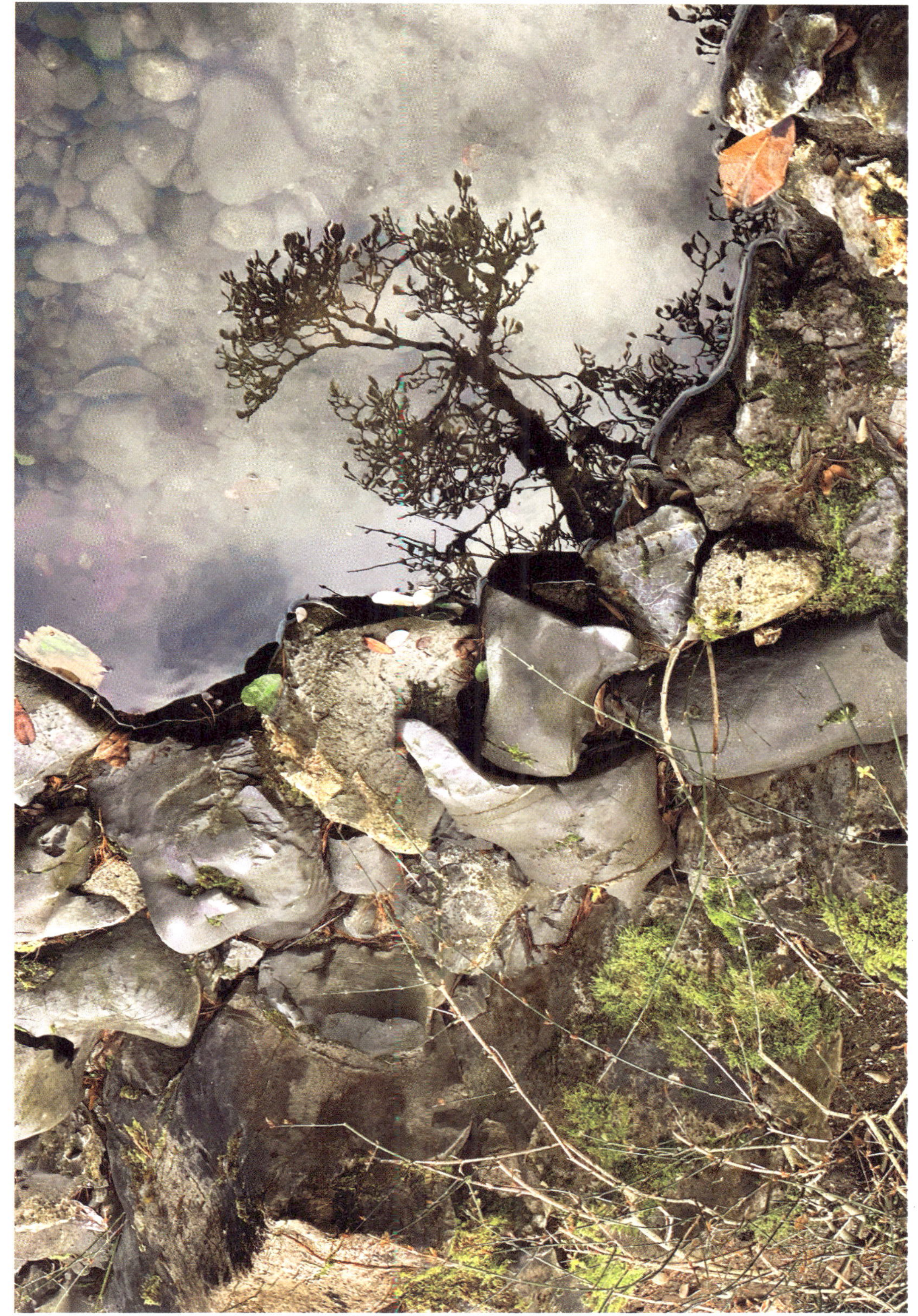

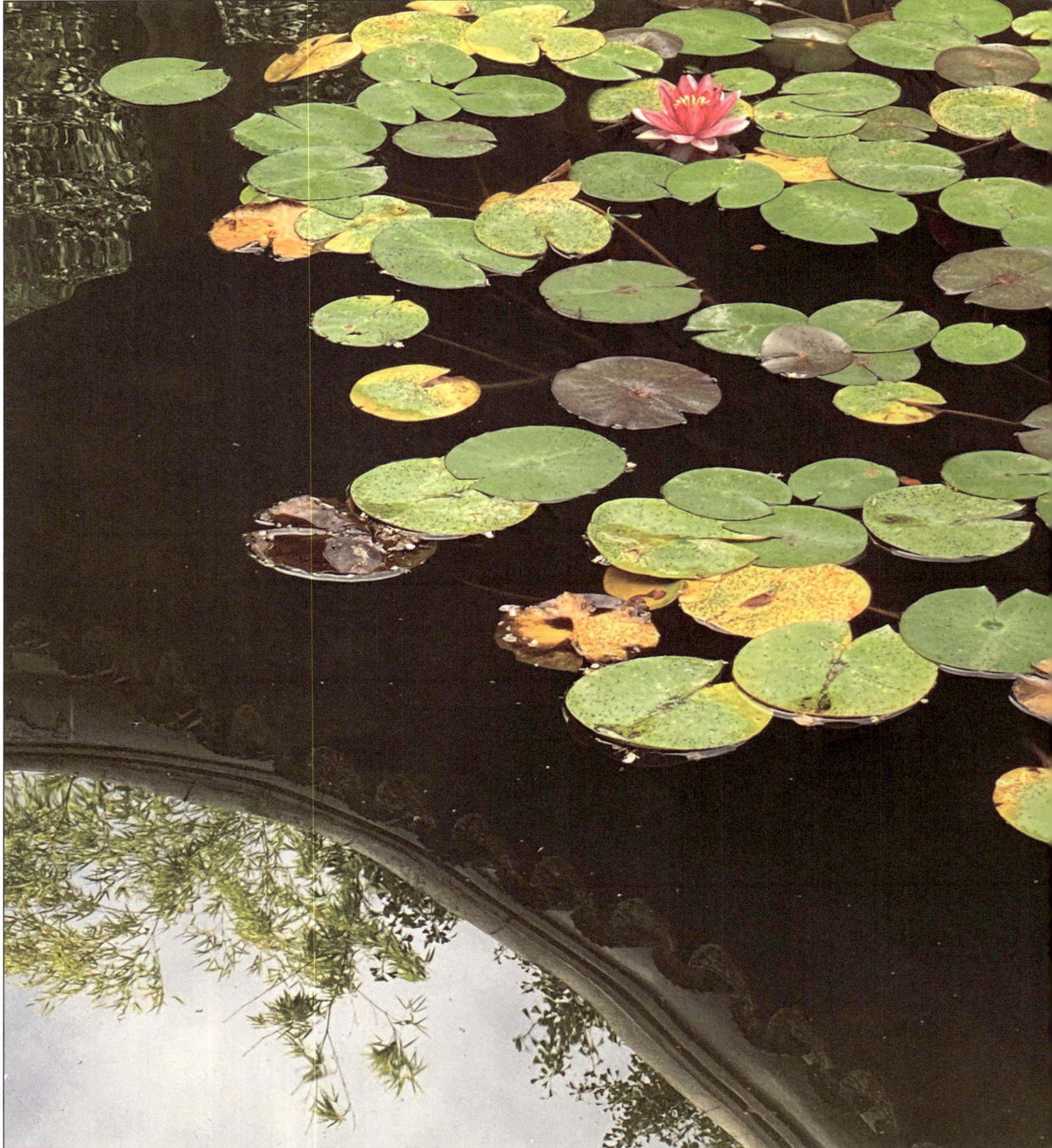

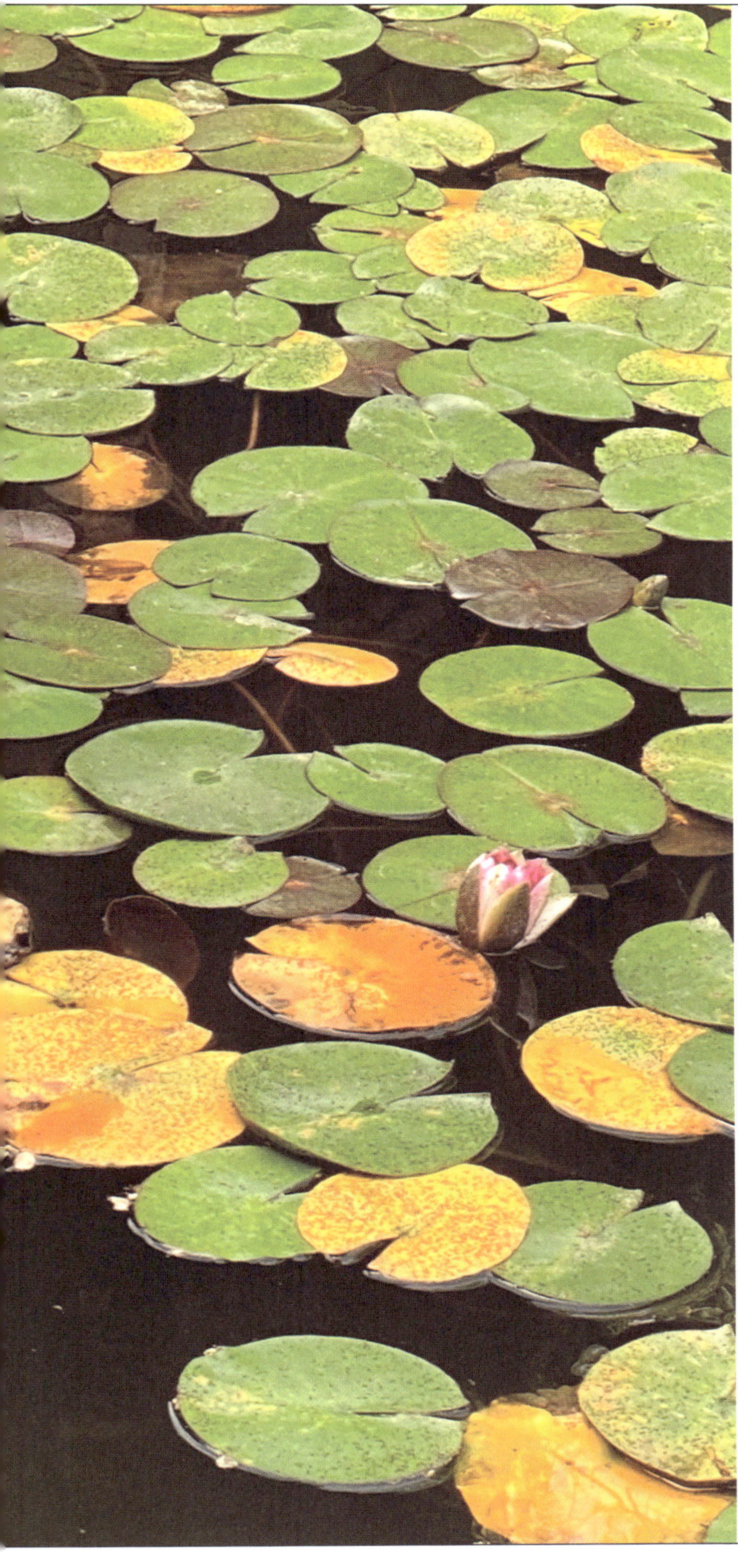

SUMMER

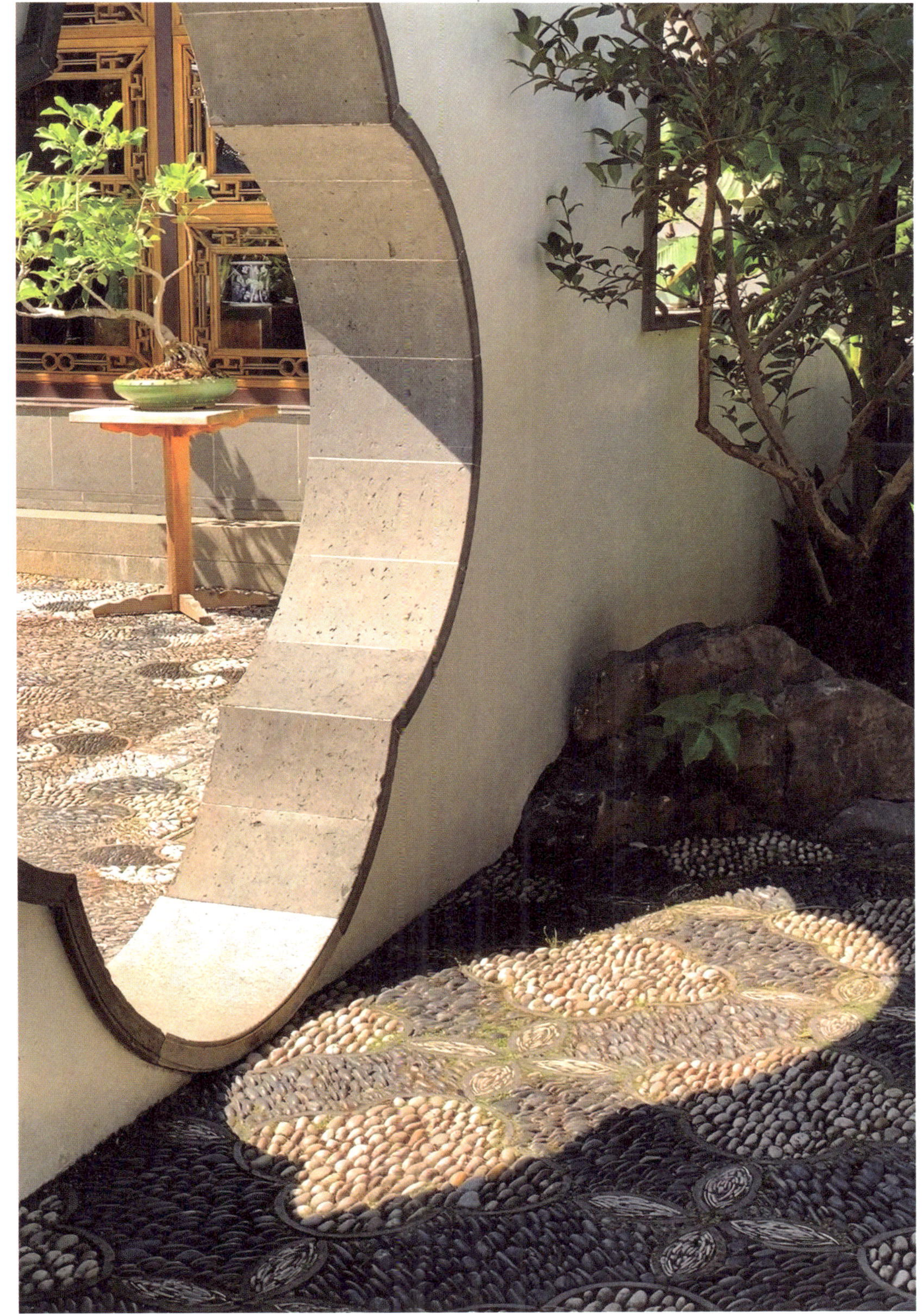

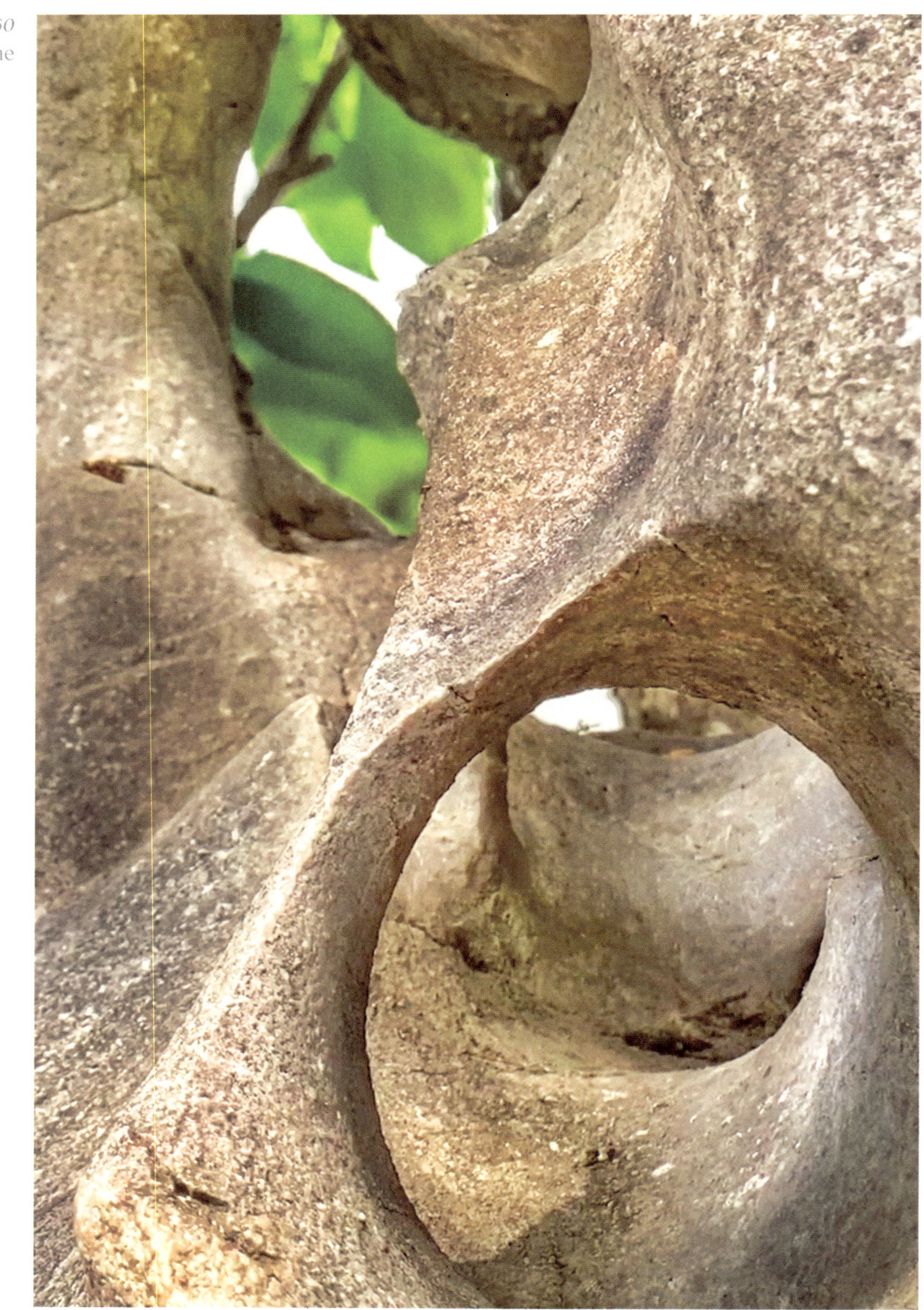

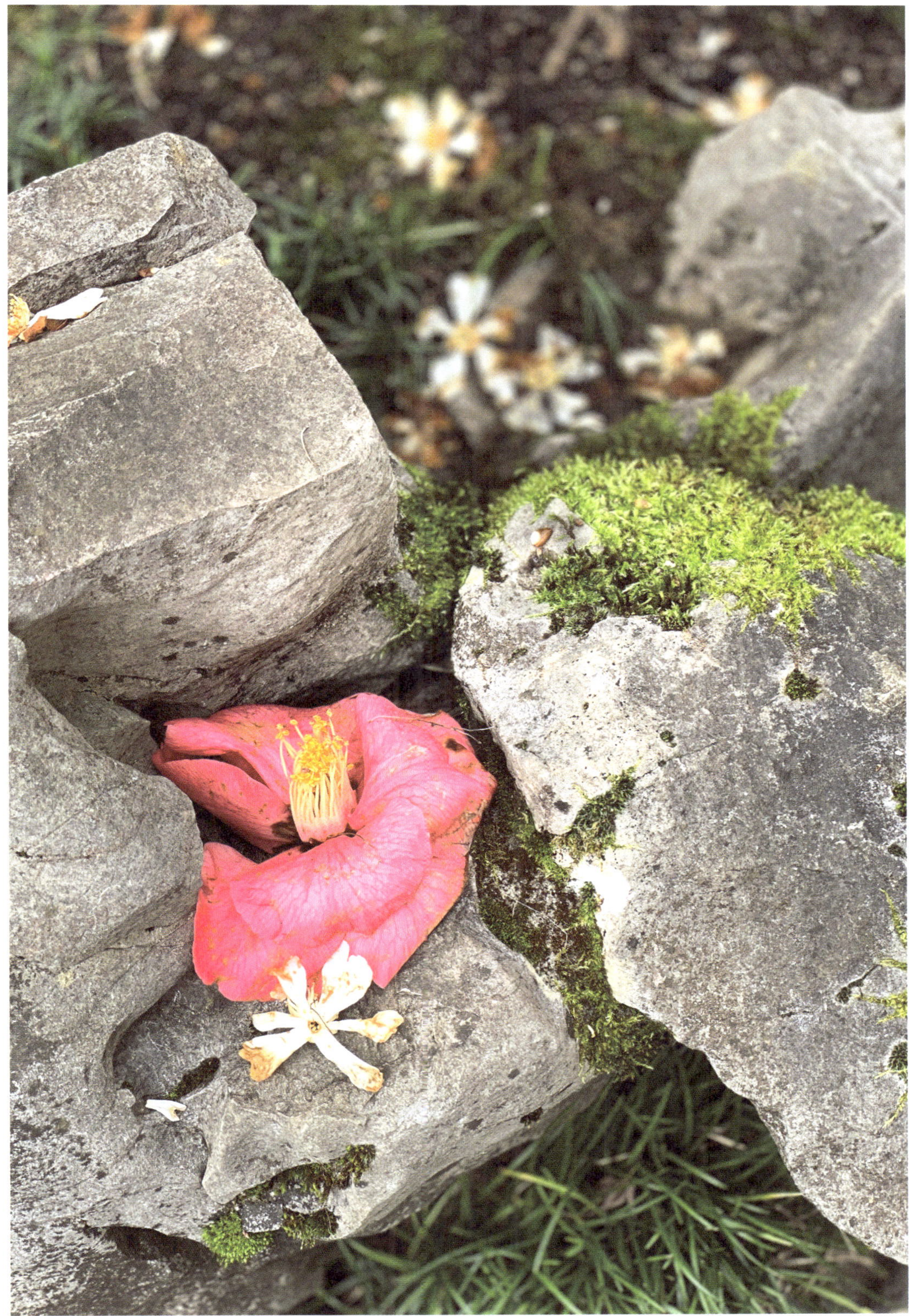

Fallen Flower

61

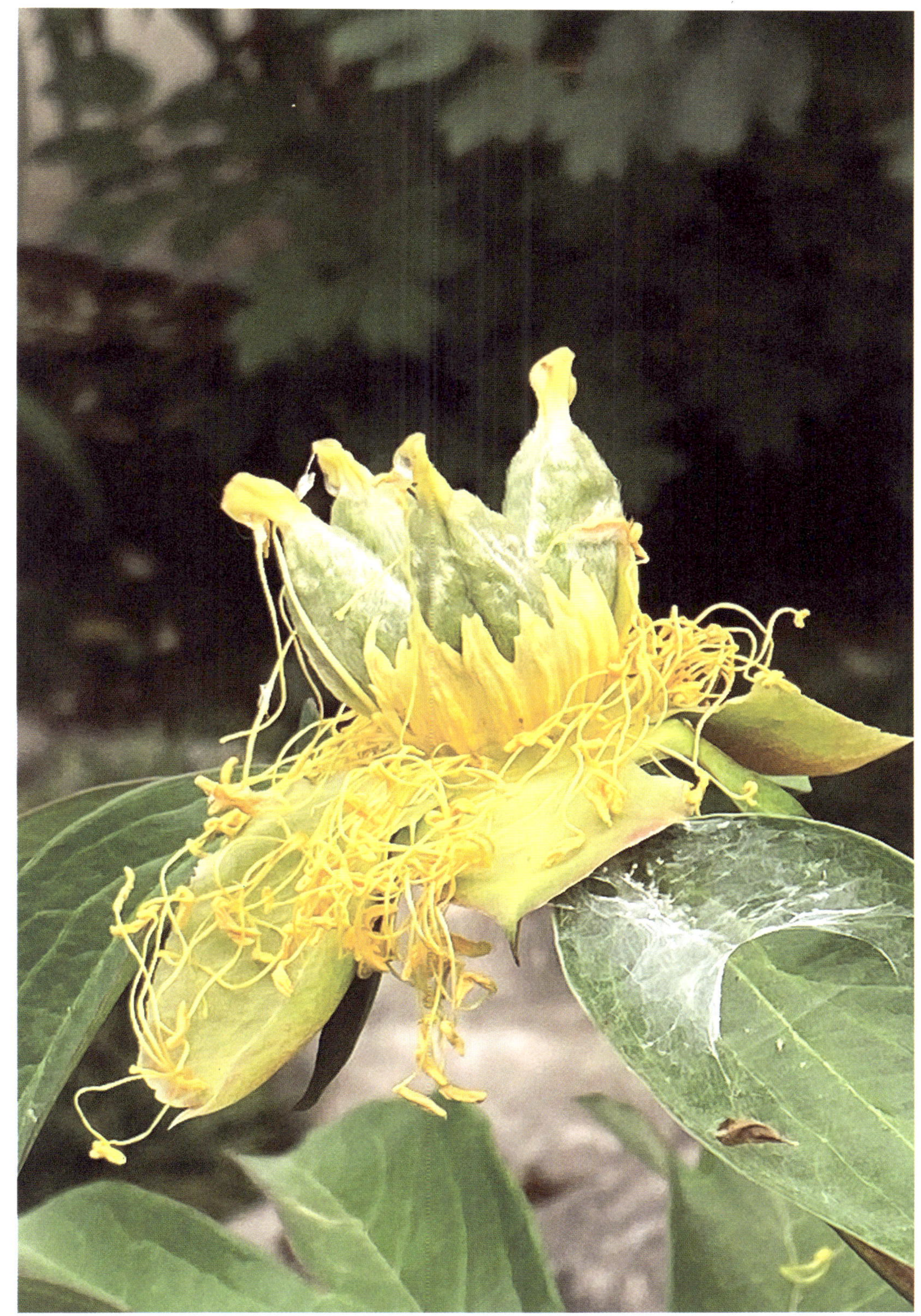

Yellow Flower

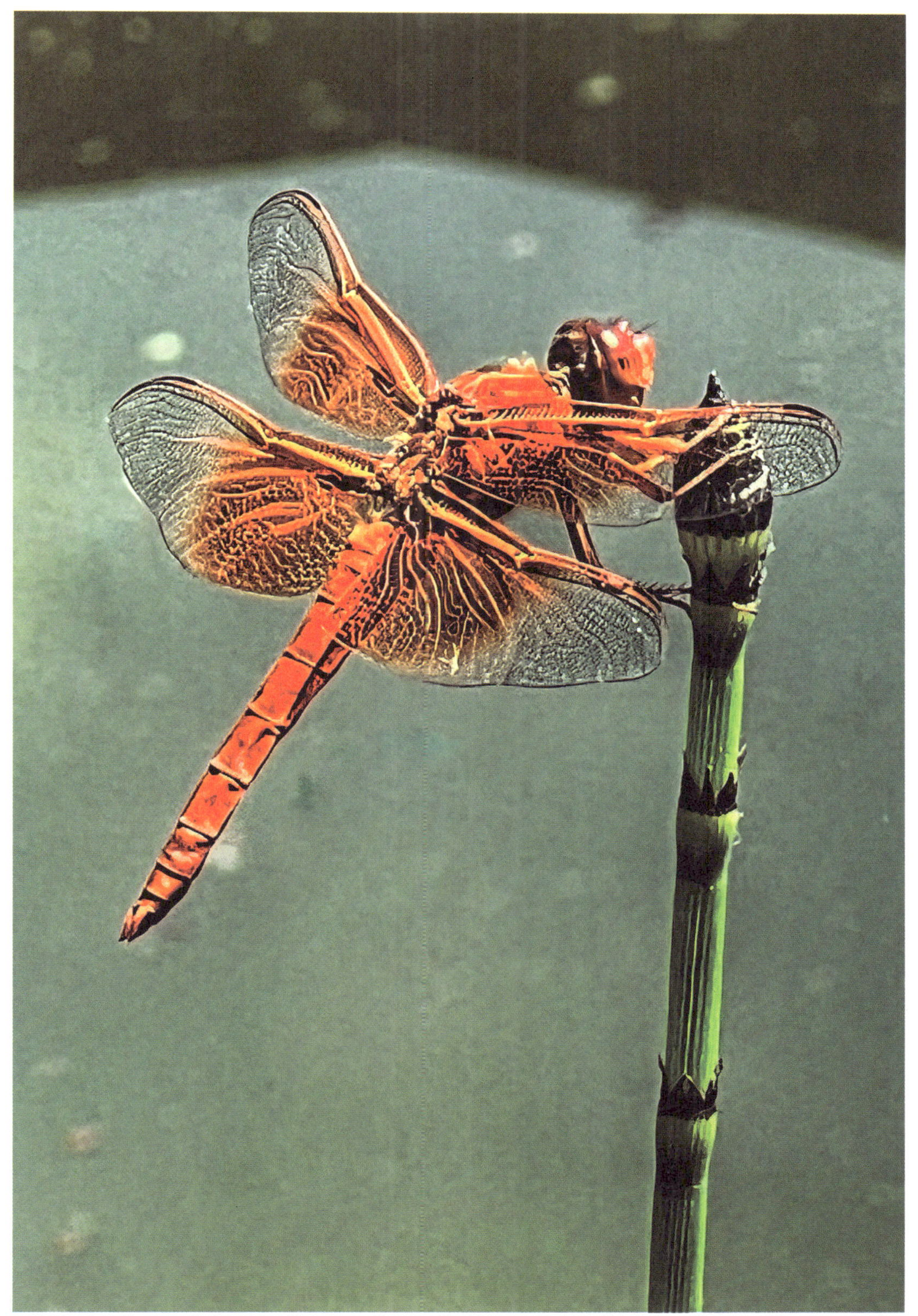

Firecracker Skimmer
65

Herringbone Floor

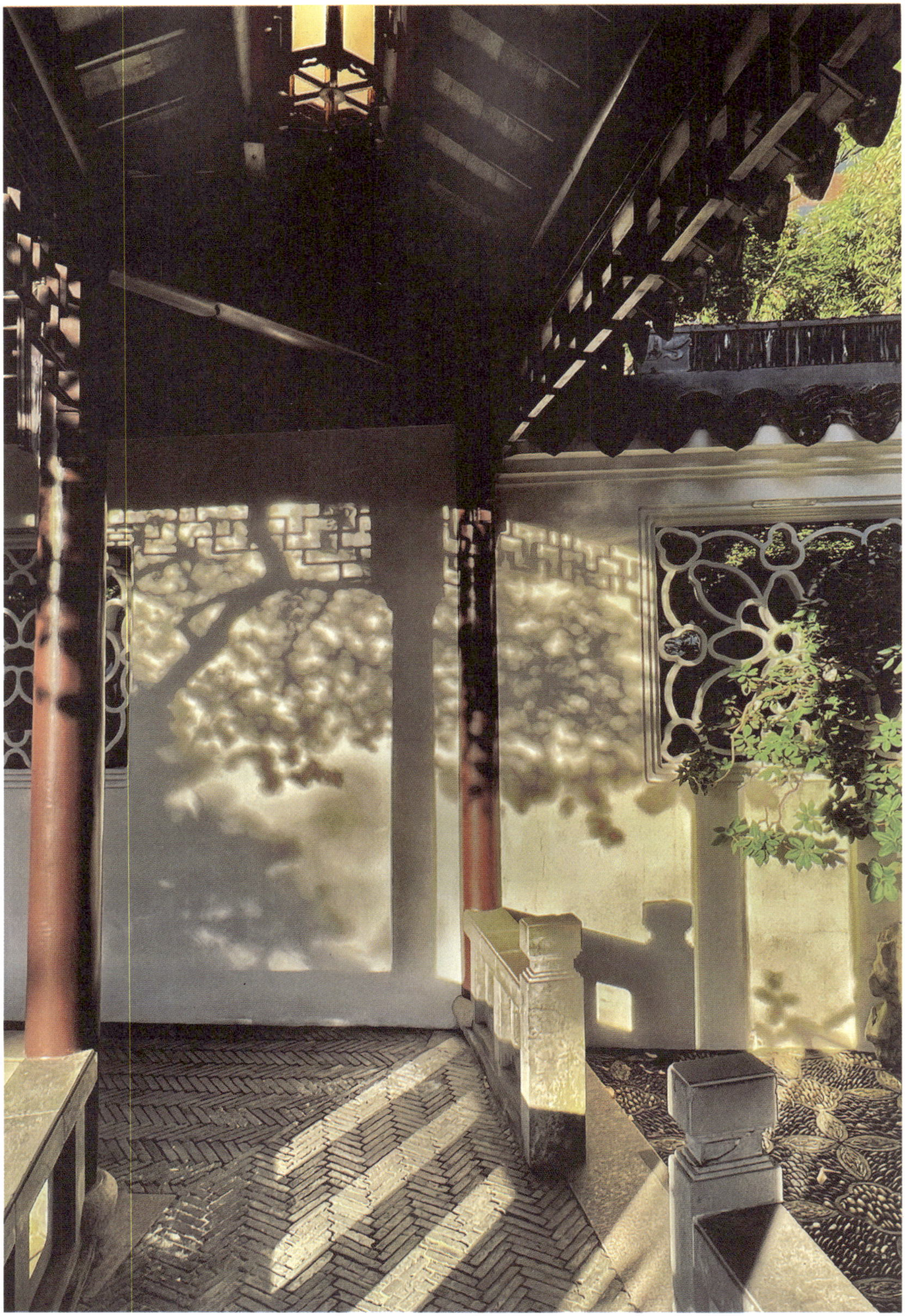

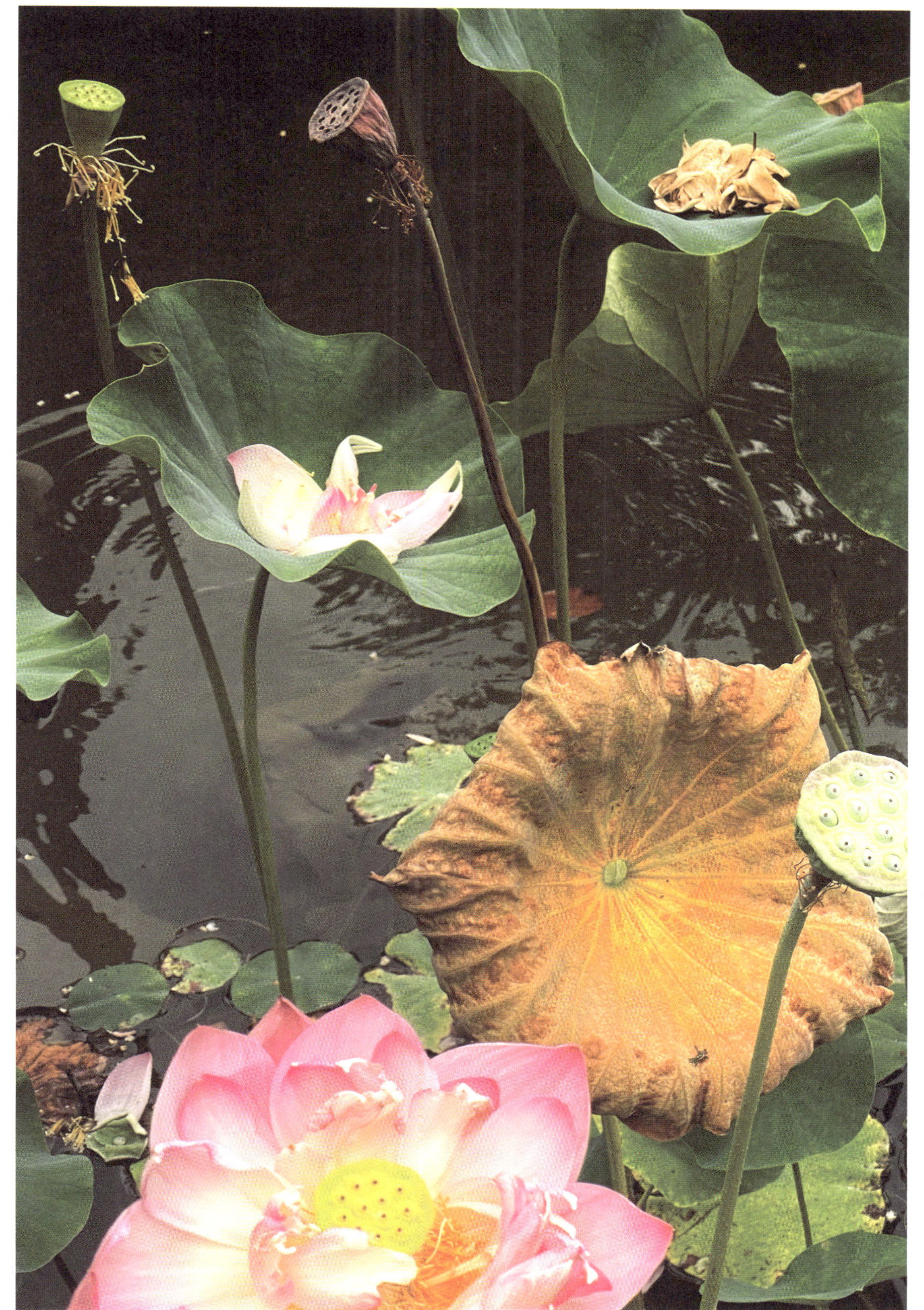

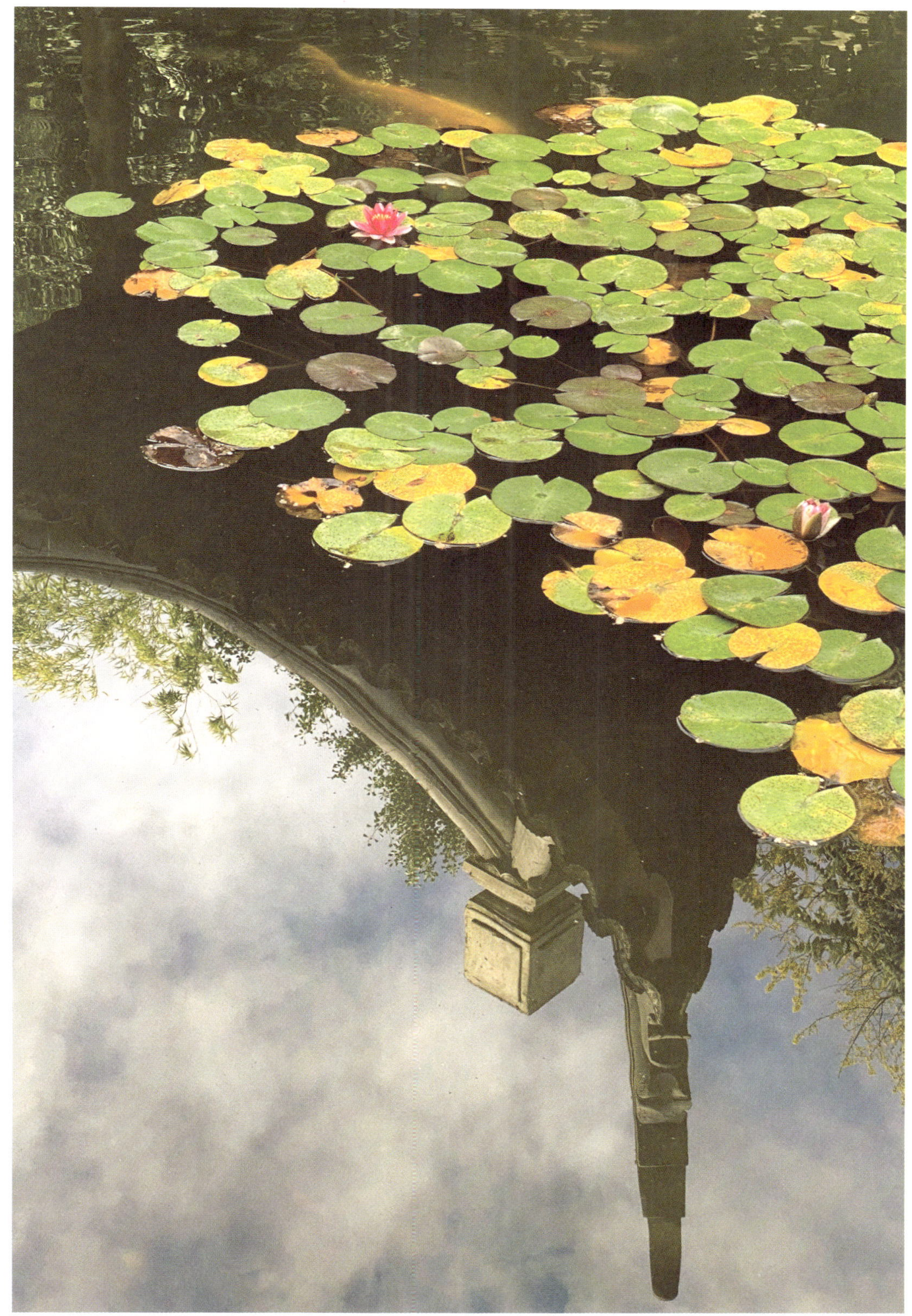

Floating

69

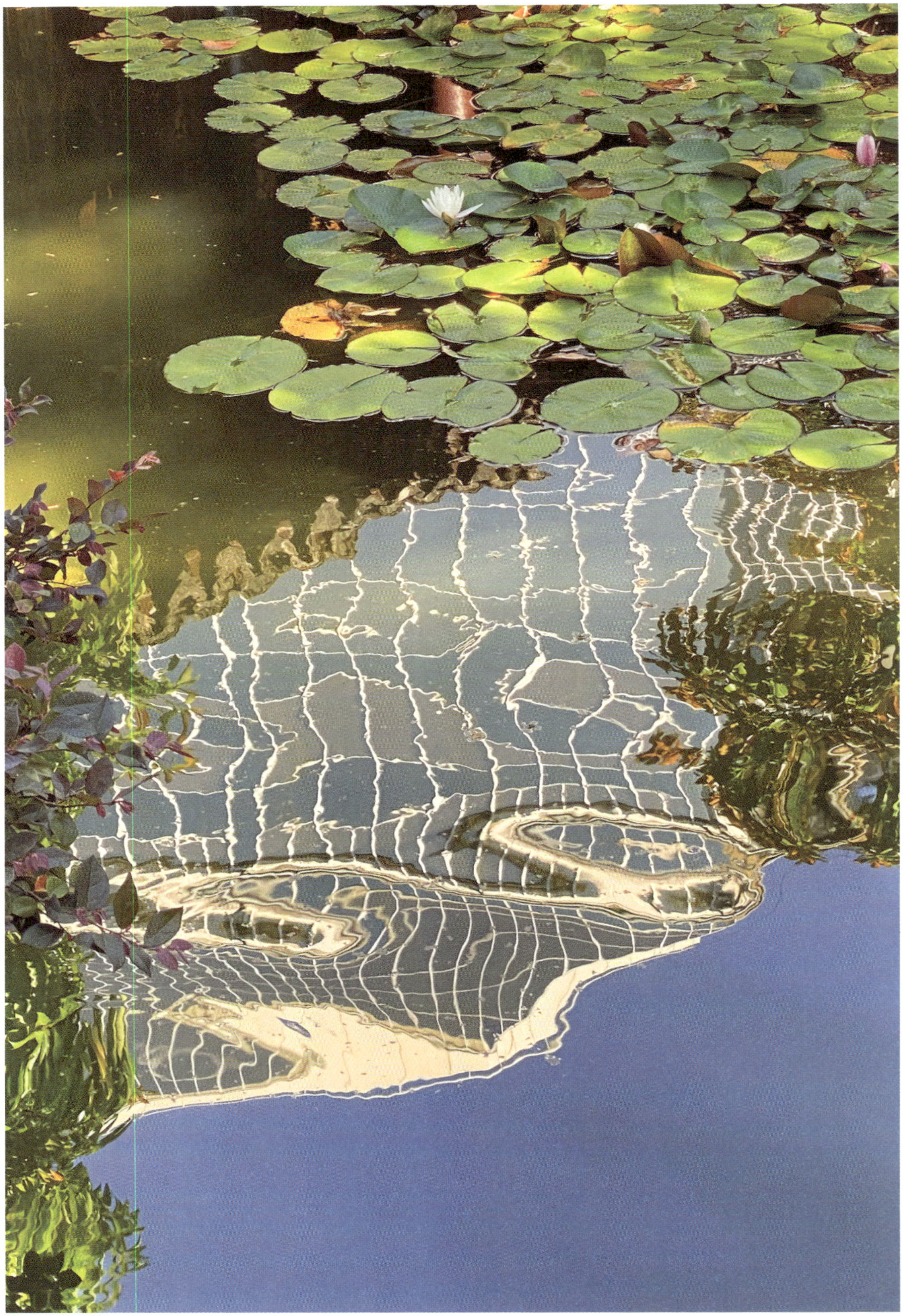

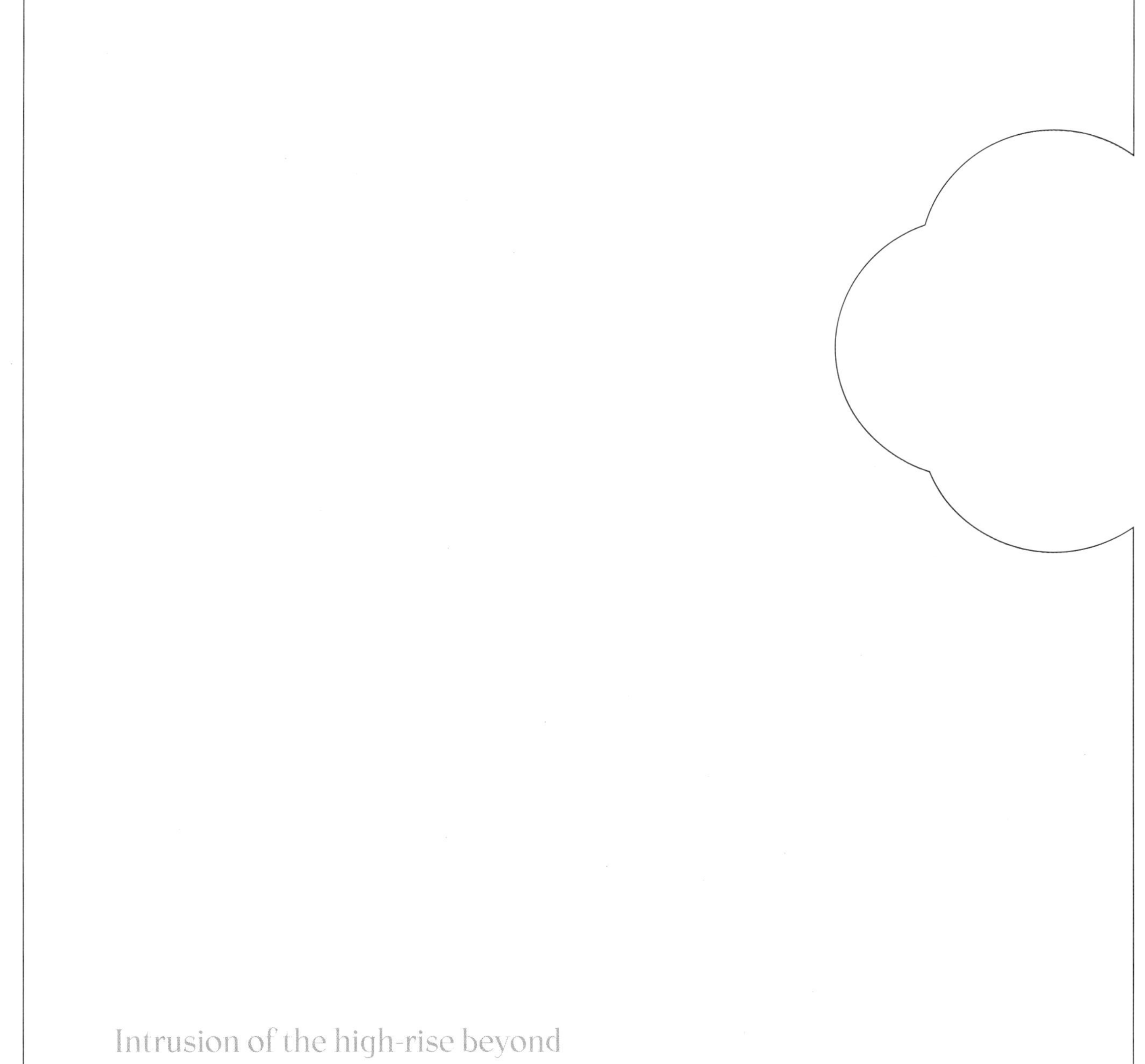

Intrusion of the high-rise beyond
The embracing walls of the Garden
Imprints itself onto the pond
An unexpected gift.

Filigree

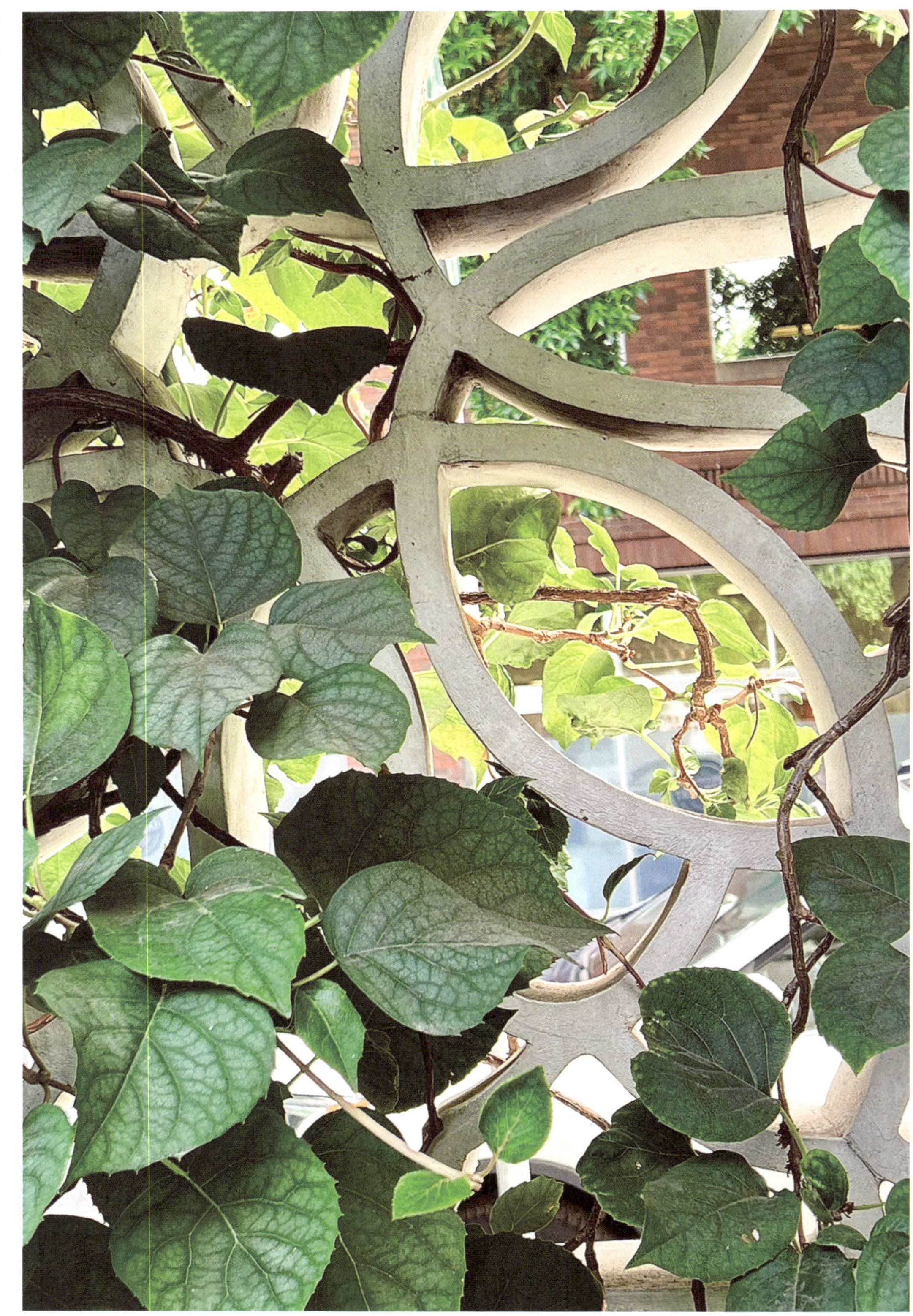

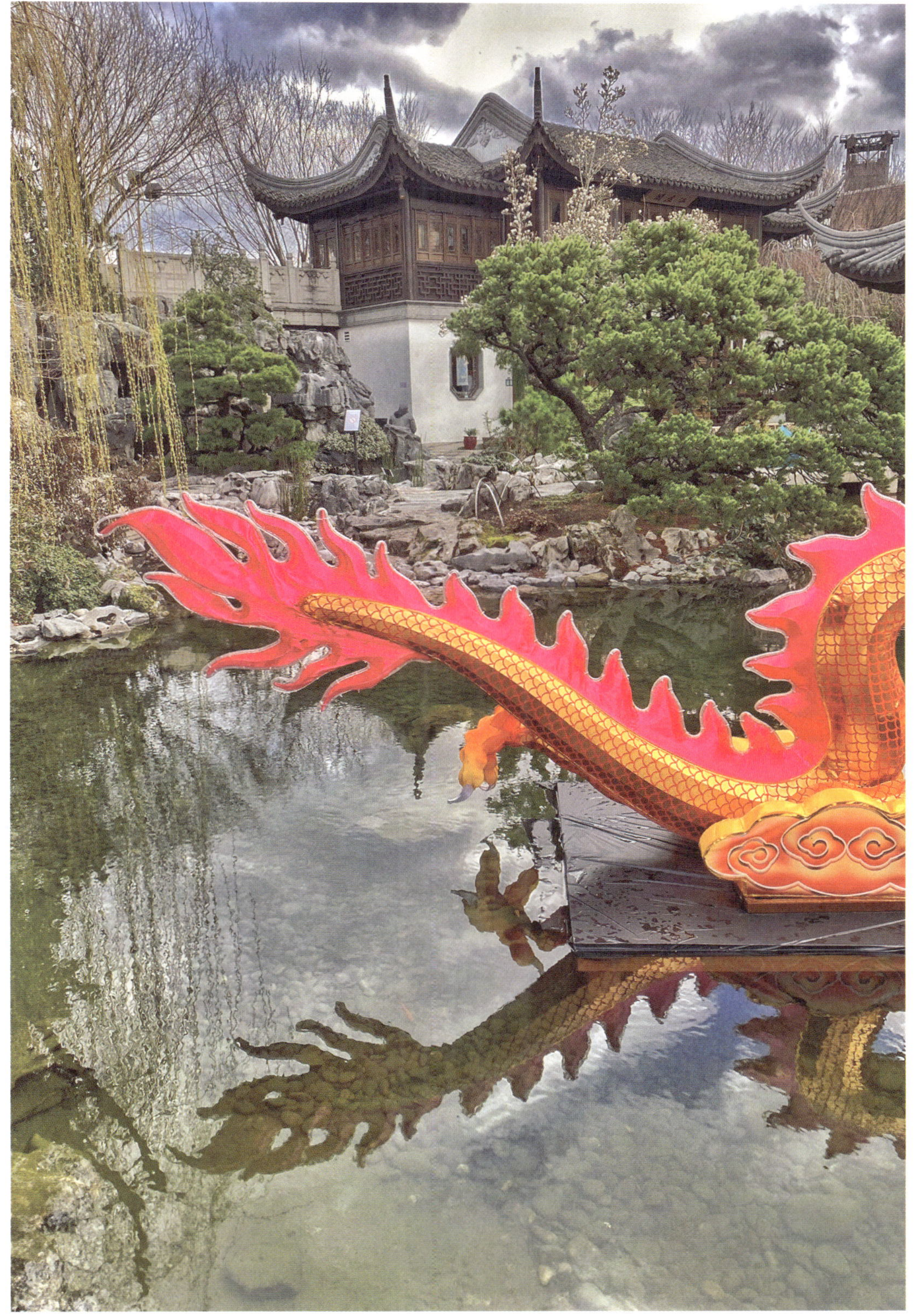

Dragon's Tail

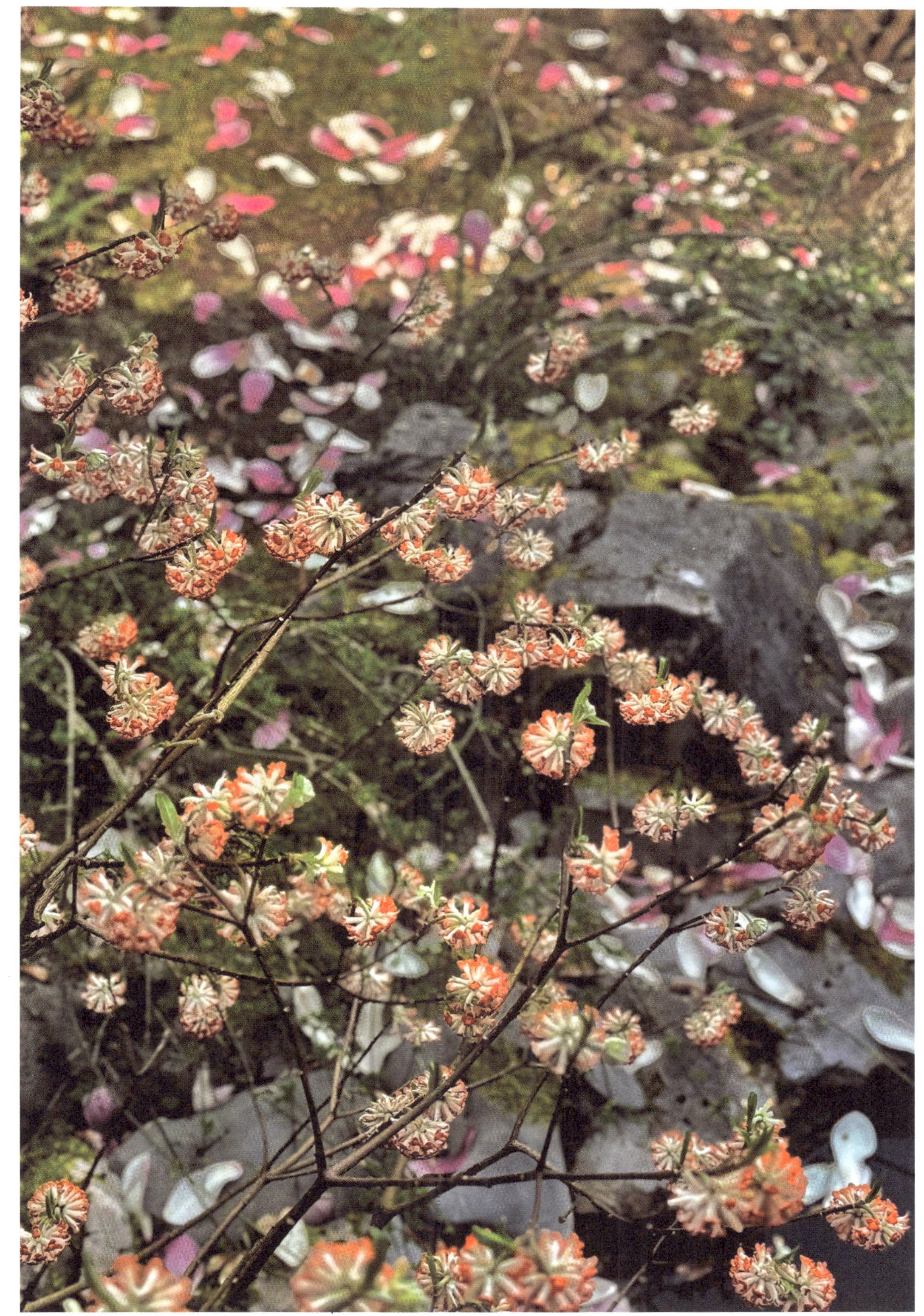

Dangling Blossoms

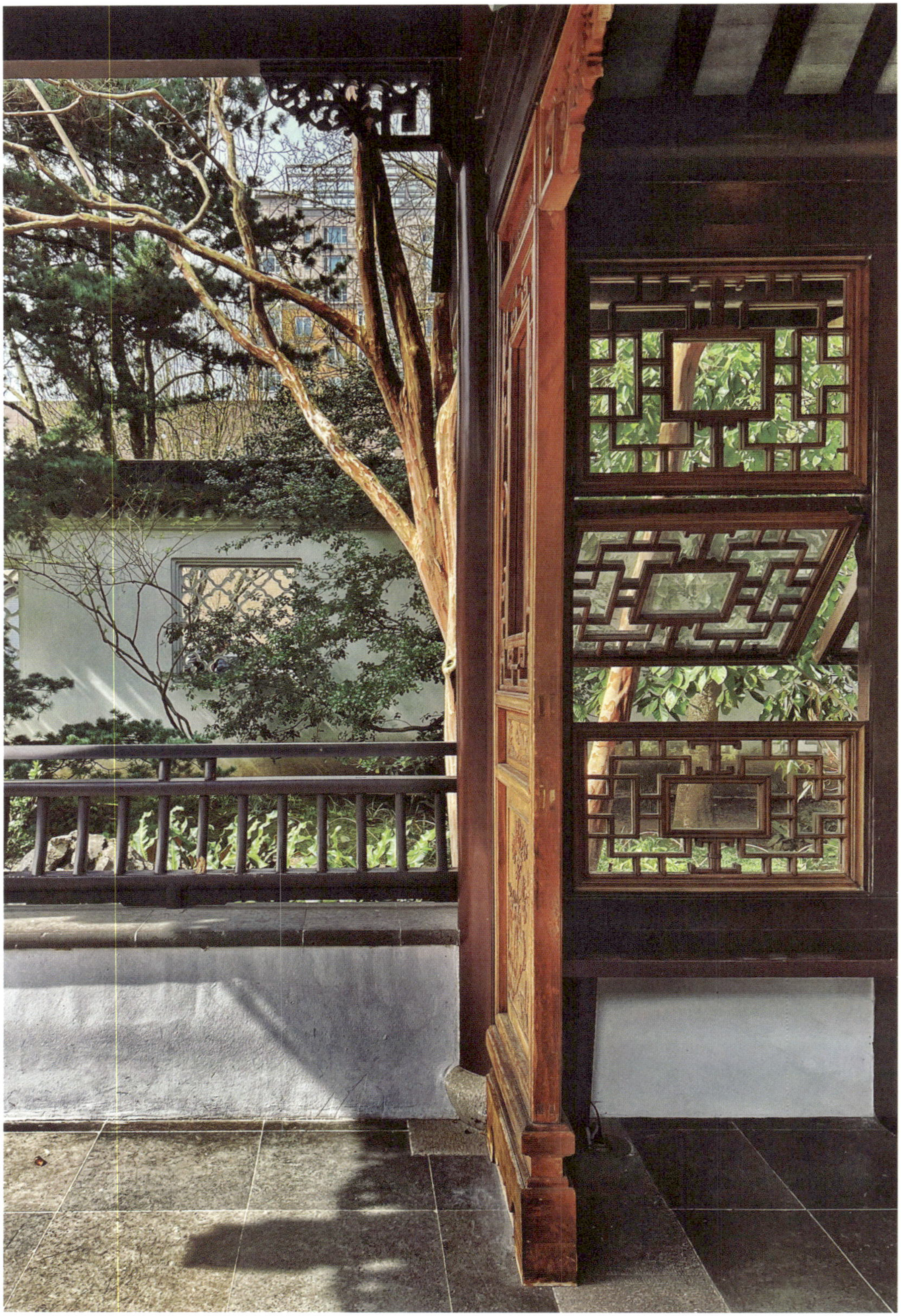

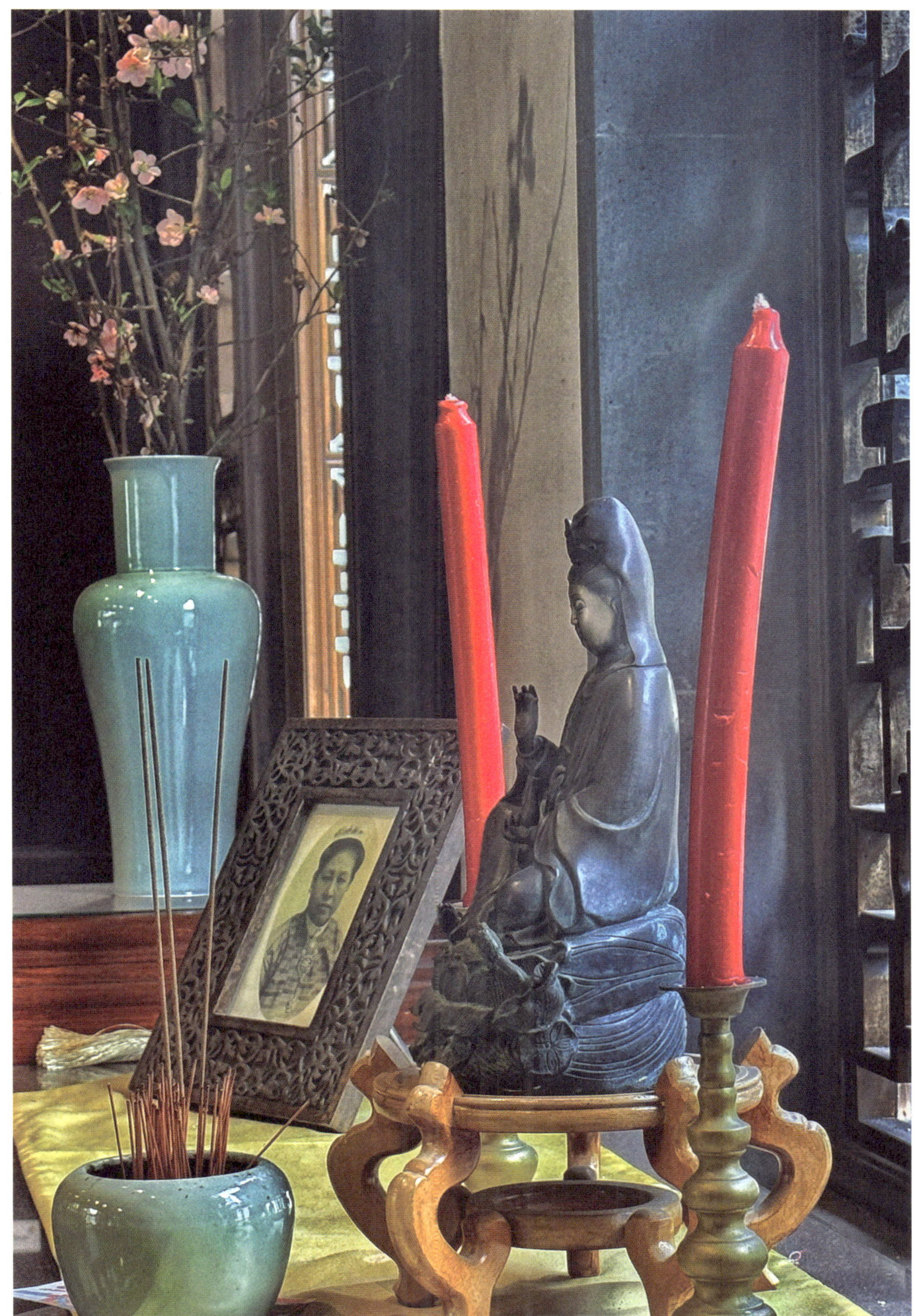

Altar

11

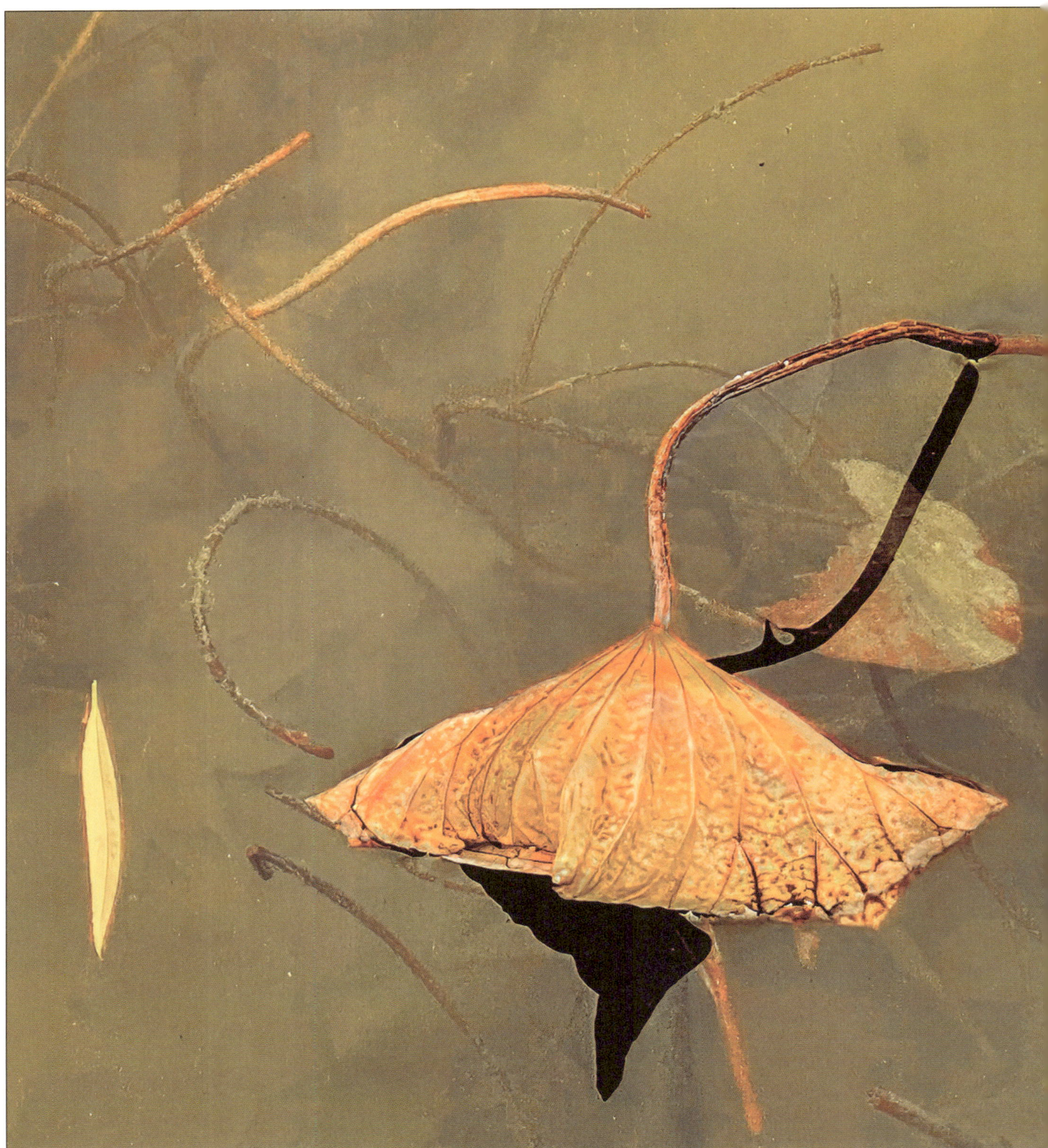

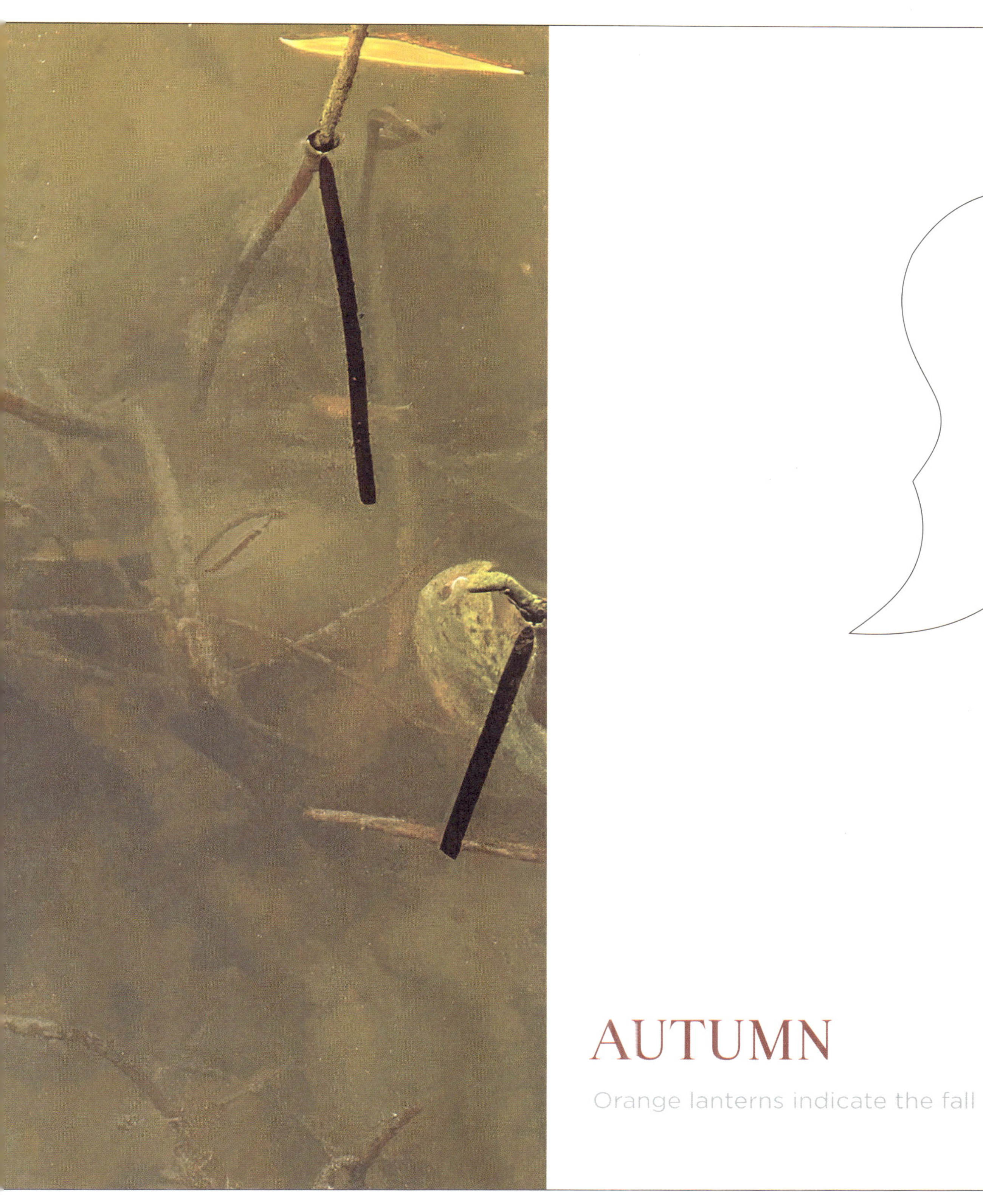

AUTUMN

Orange lanterns indicate the fall

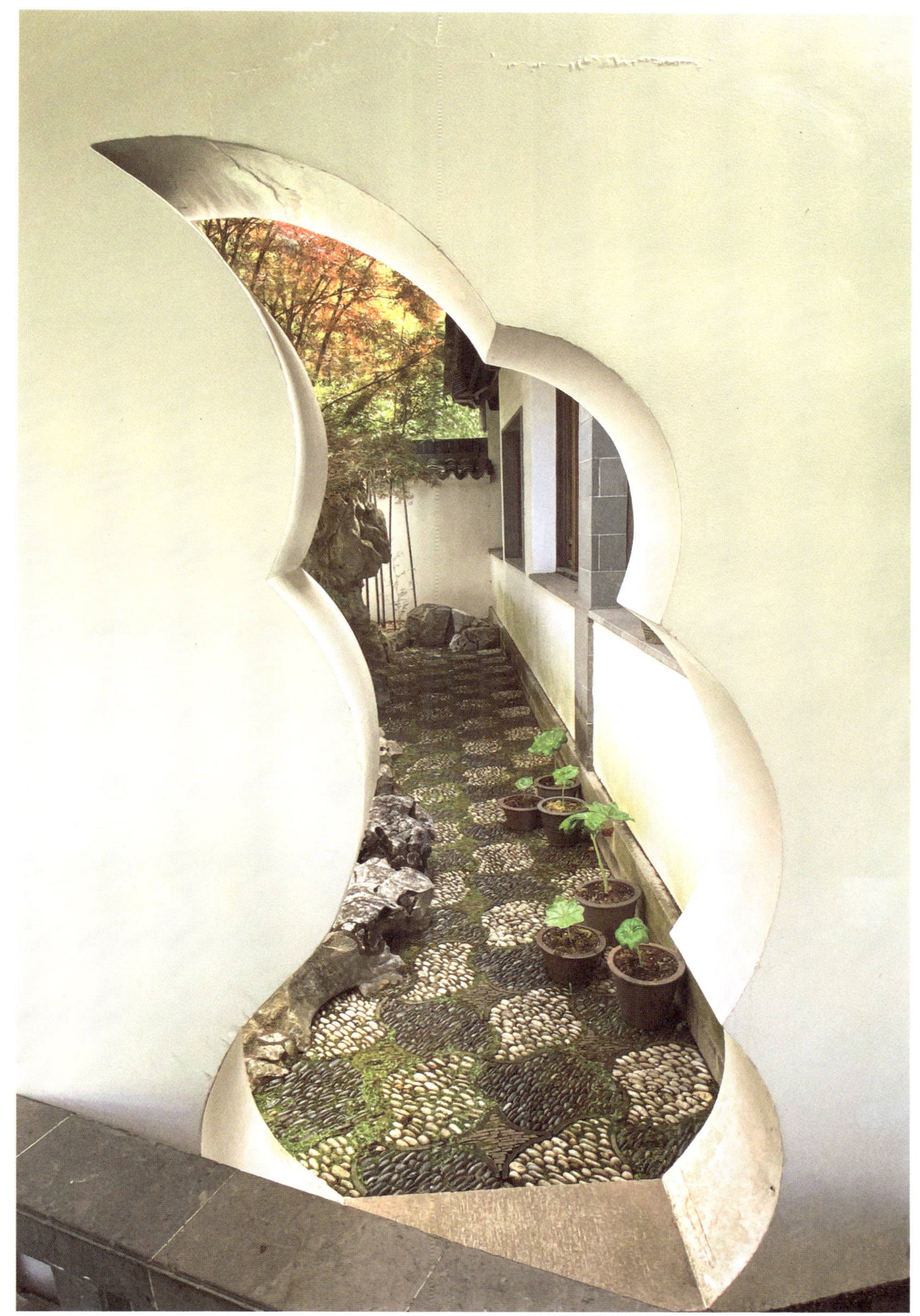

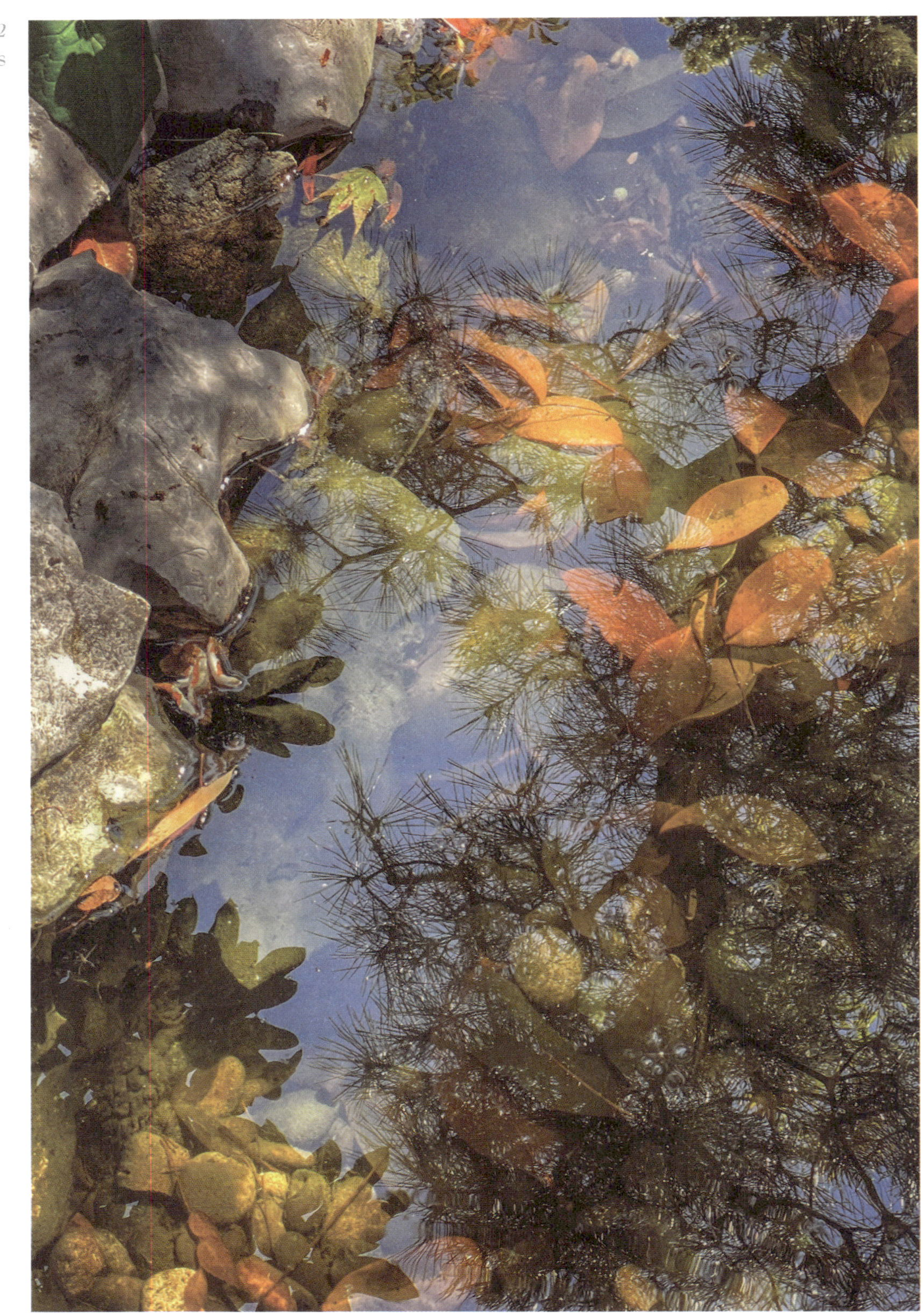

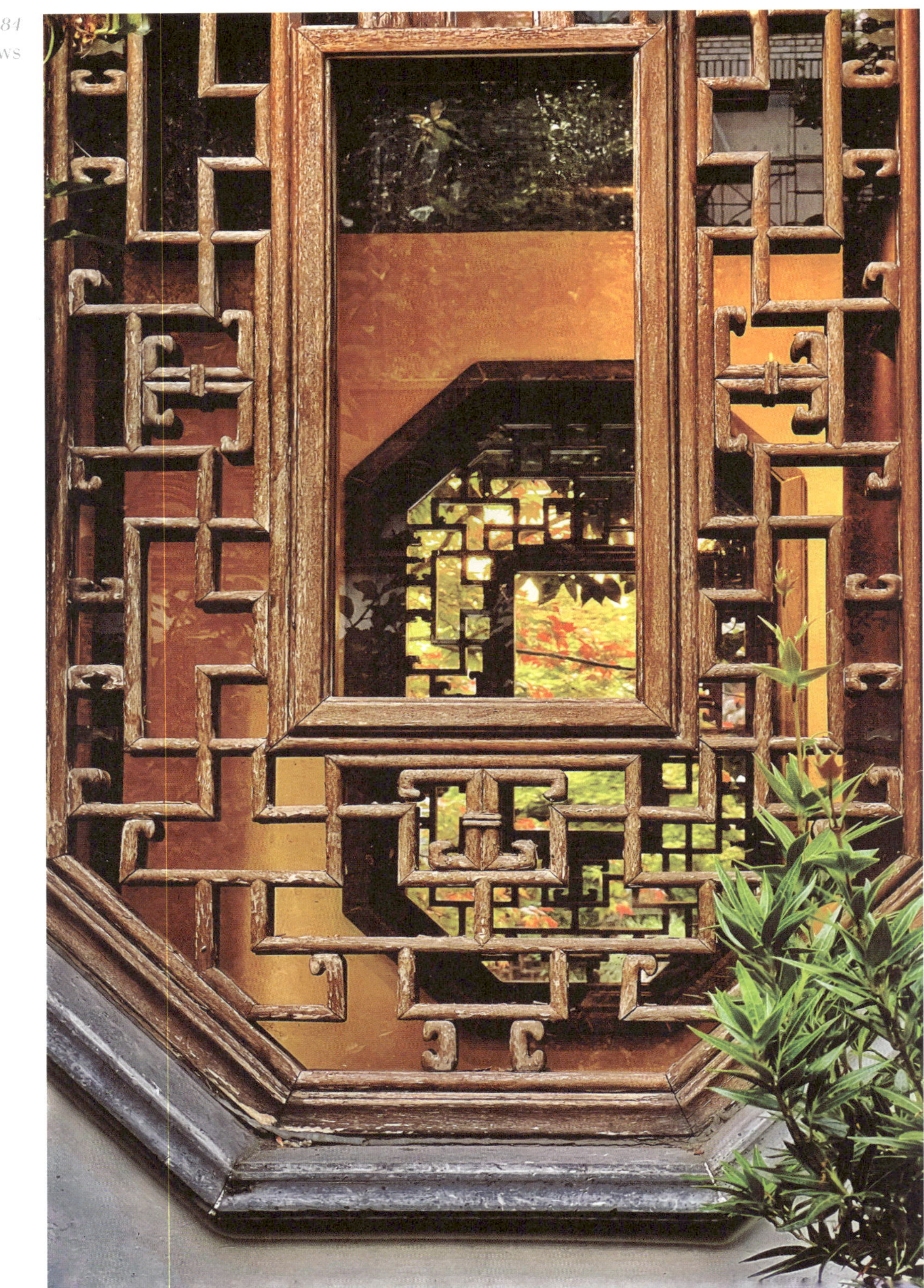

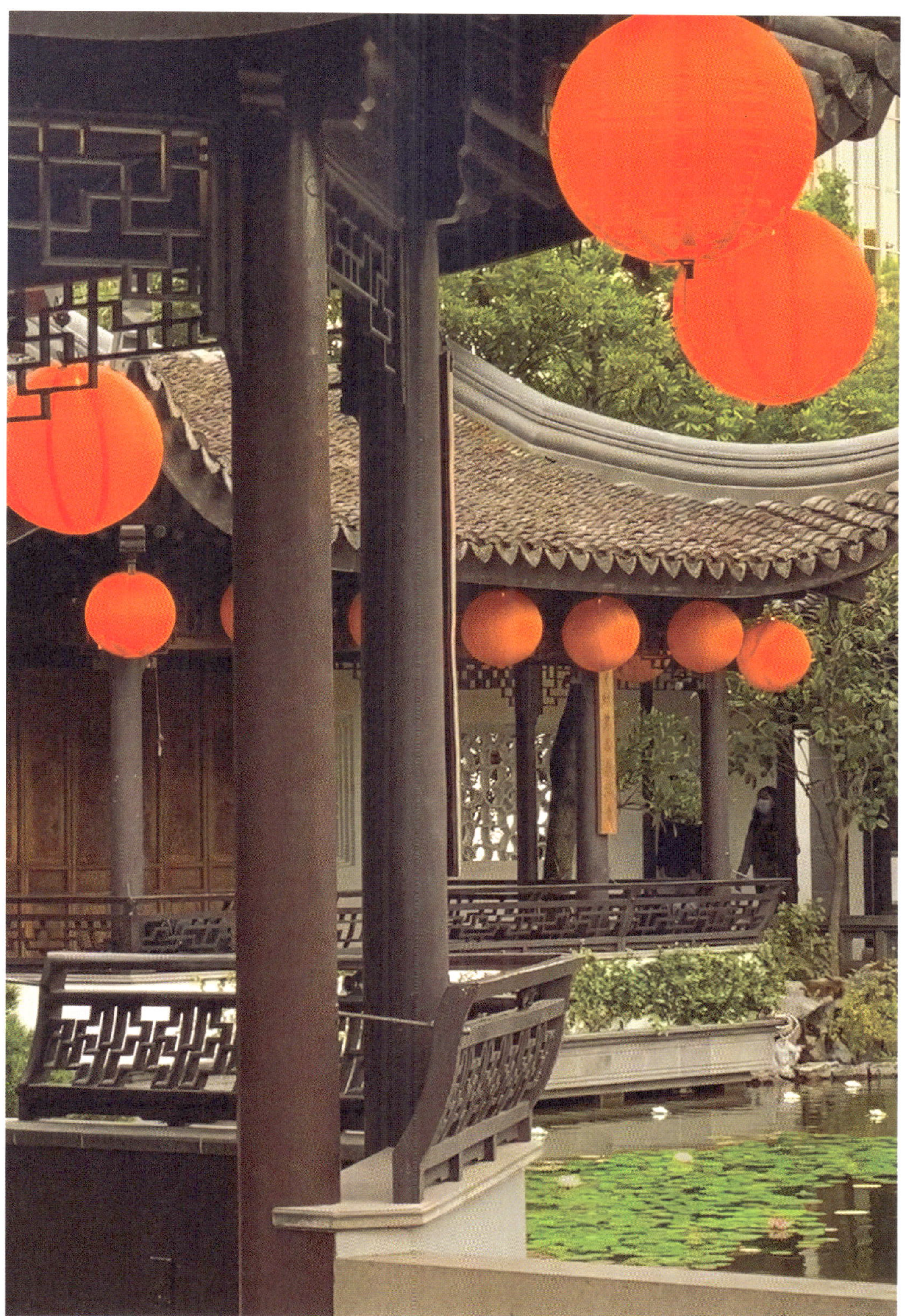

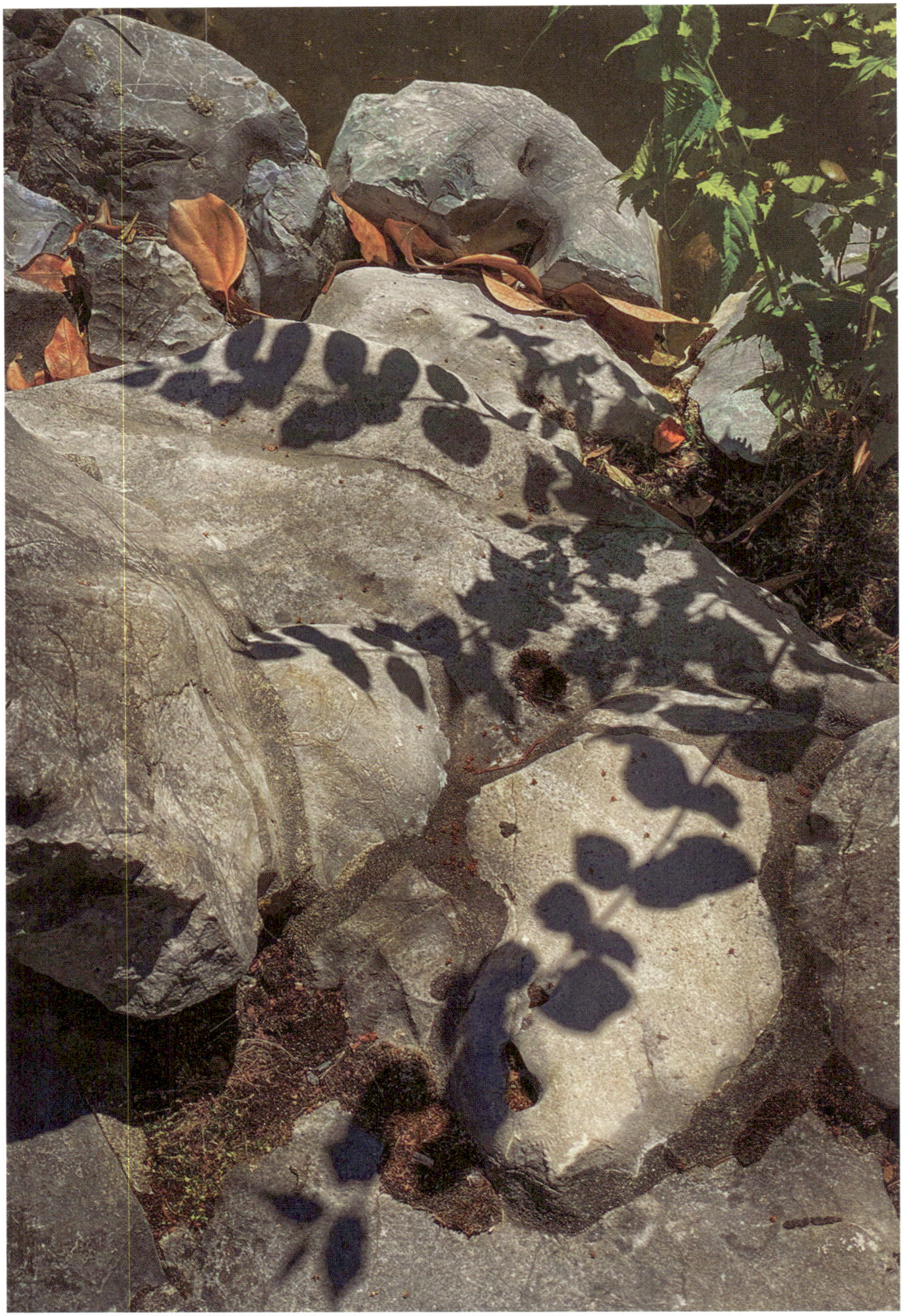

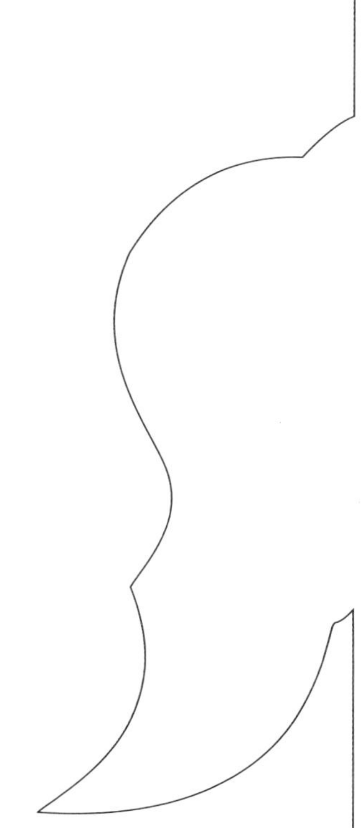

I sit by the open window in the Tea House.

Fragrant steam from my cup of ginger tea

warms me. Outside, the rain has stopped

but still drips from the golden leaves

of the Weeping Katsura tree, befitting

its name. An hour ago I stood

on the bridge that stretches

over the small pond and watched

a bright orange koi swish

through the water as if preparing

for winter. Then the rain began,

blurring my view. The poet Tu Fu

writes, A good rain knows its season.

The seasons pass. The garden renews.

I grow older.

—Andrea Hollander

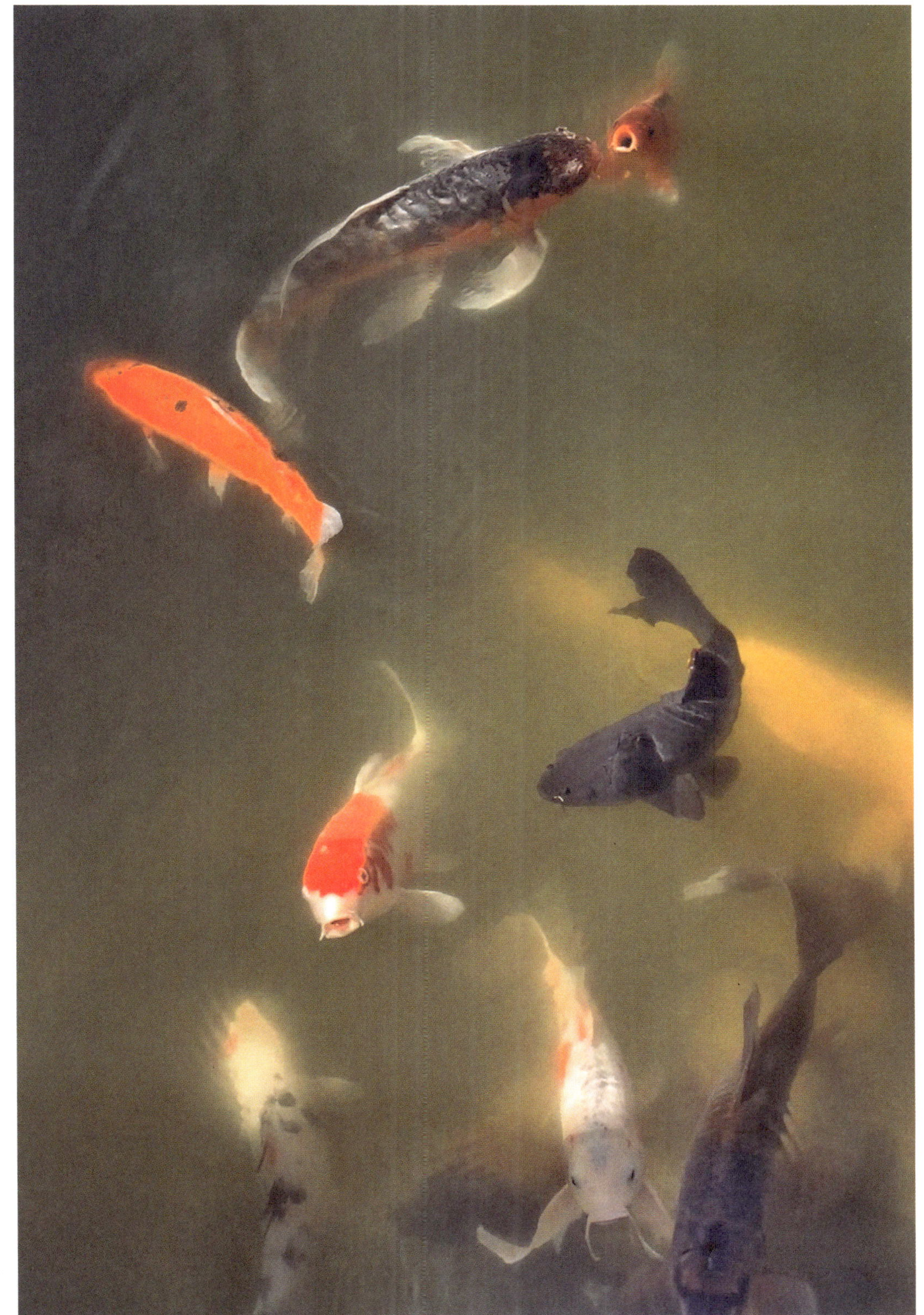

Koi (*Jin Li*) Swarm -
Koi fish represent
"Profound Virtues"

Horsetail with
Autumn Leaves

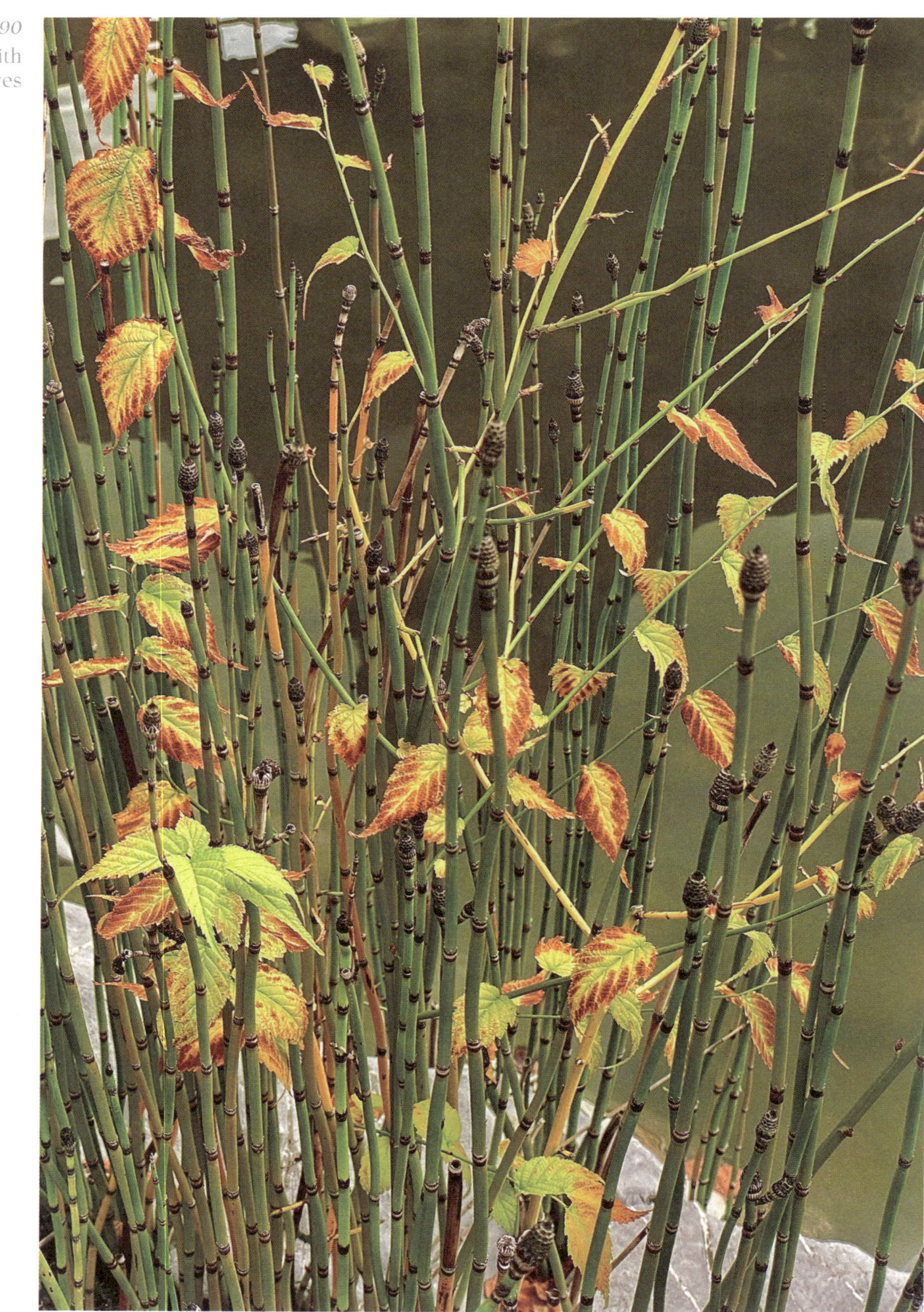

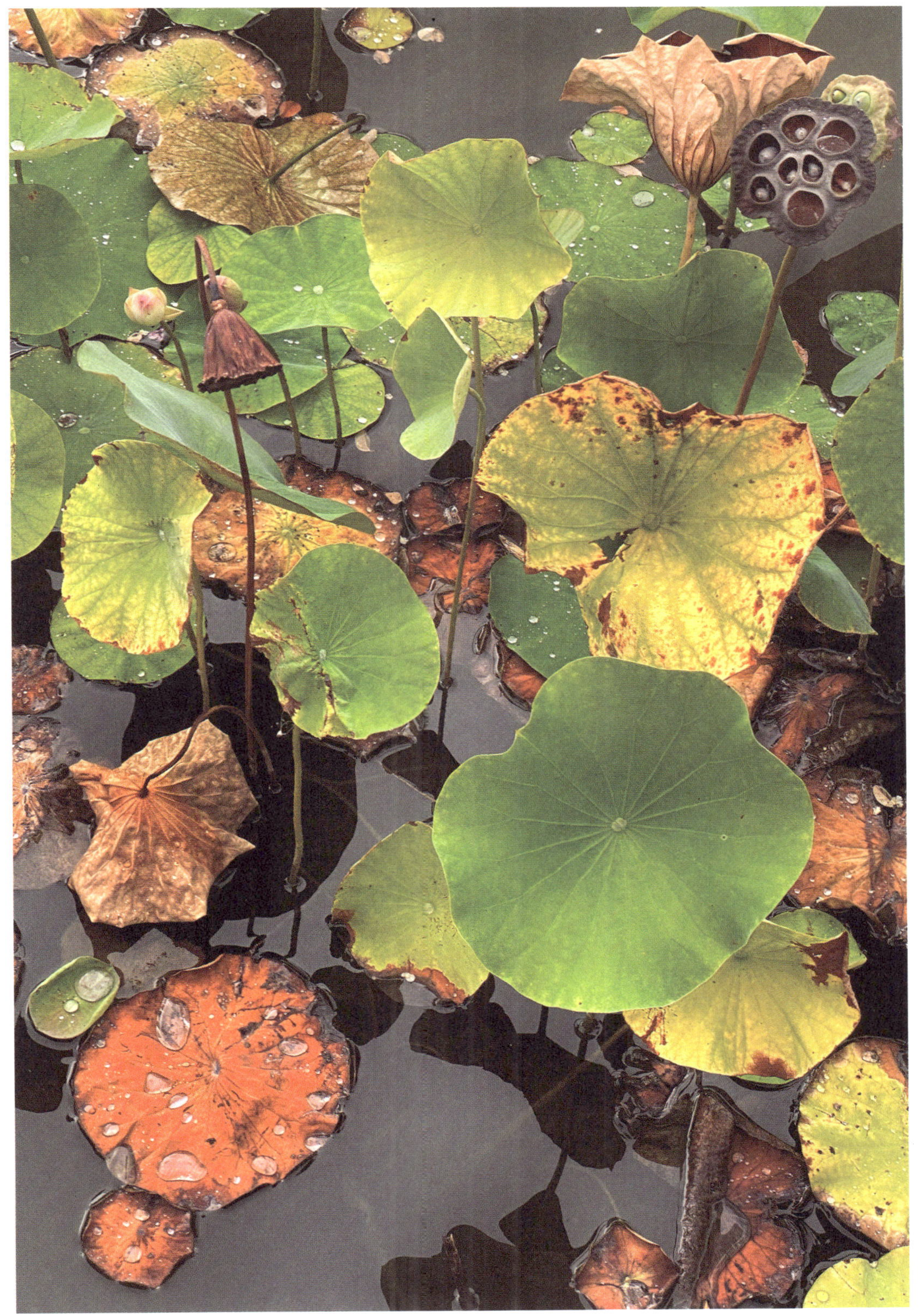

Autumn Floating
in Pond

91

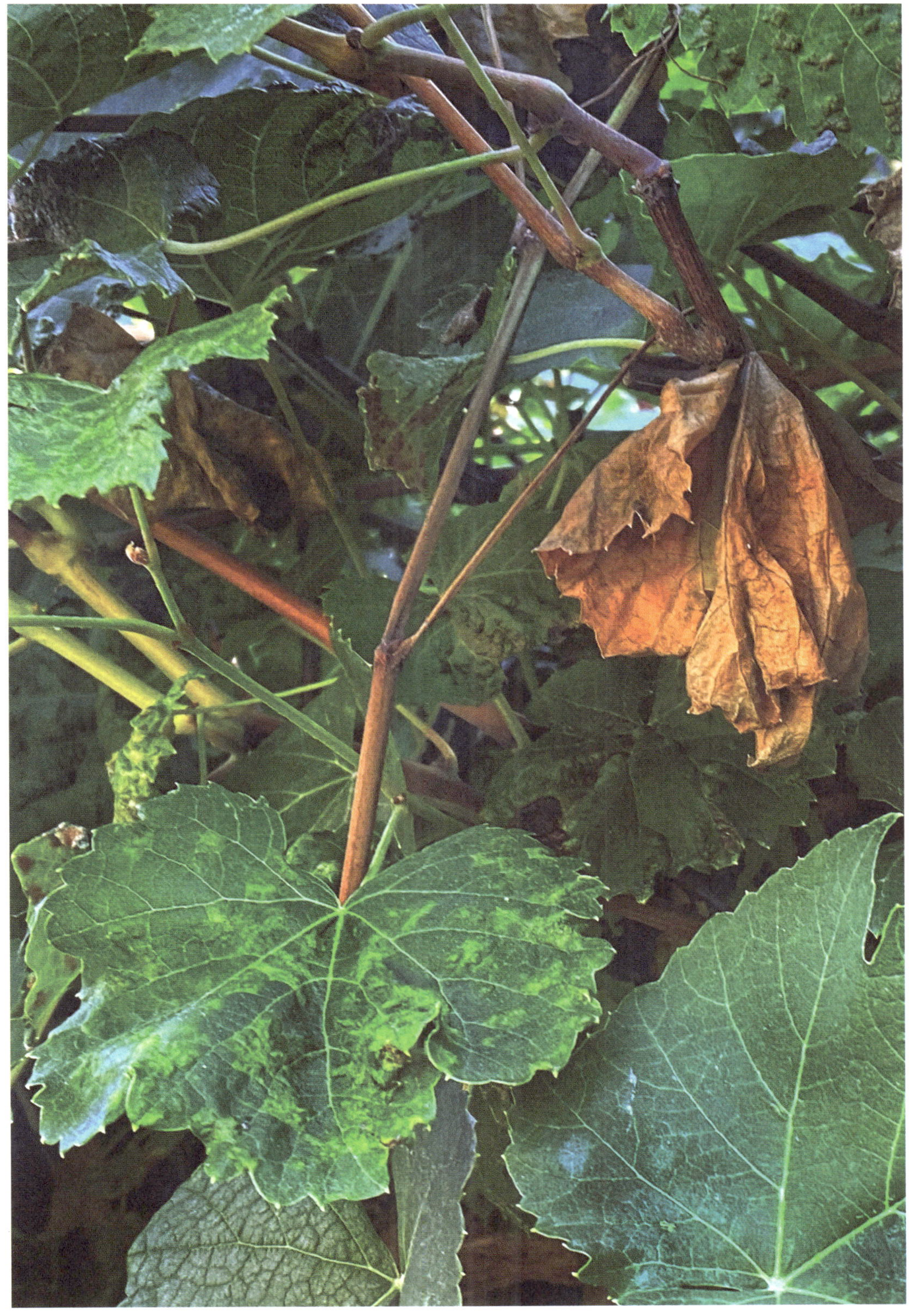

Autumn Leaf

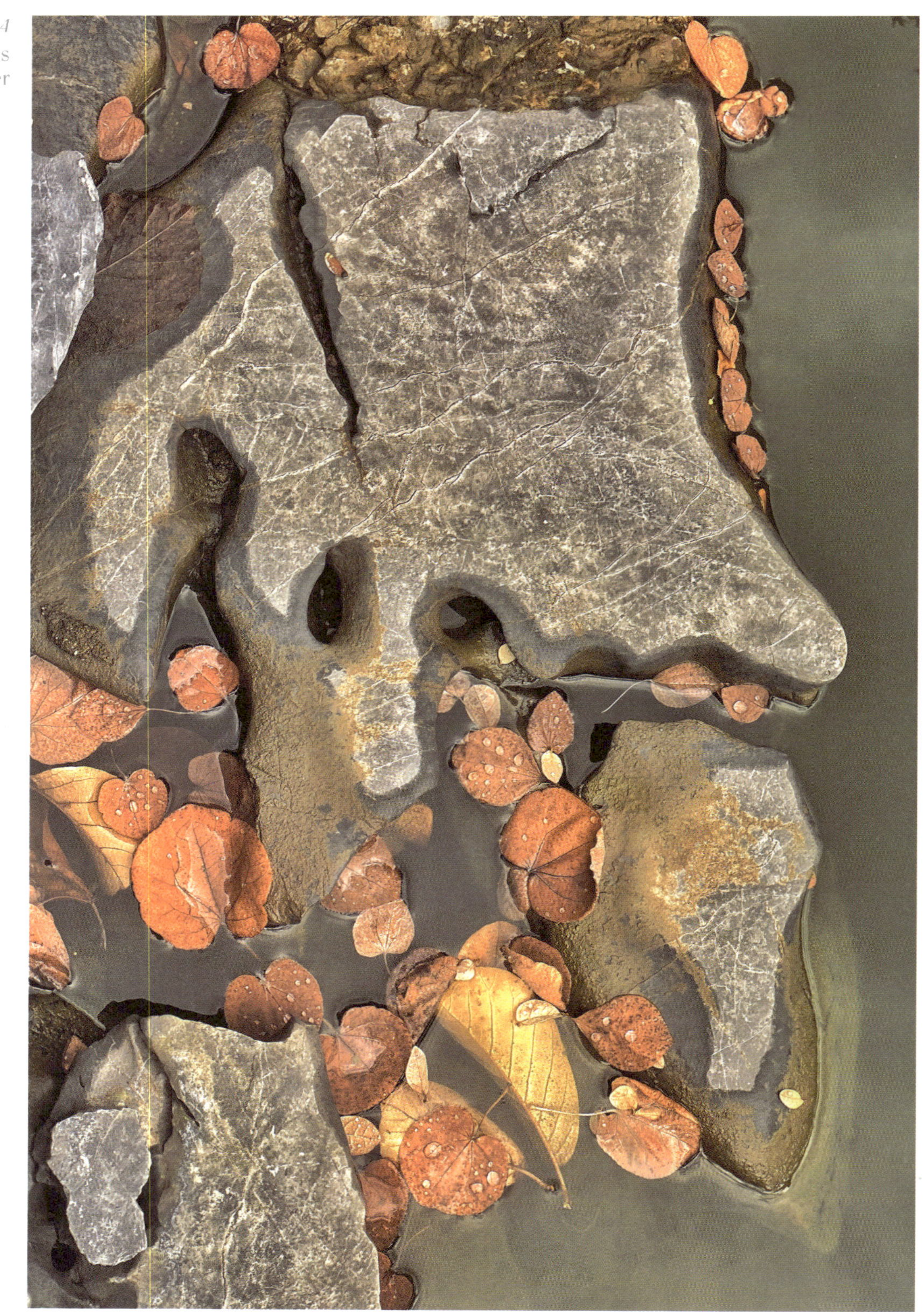

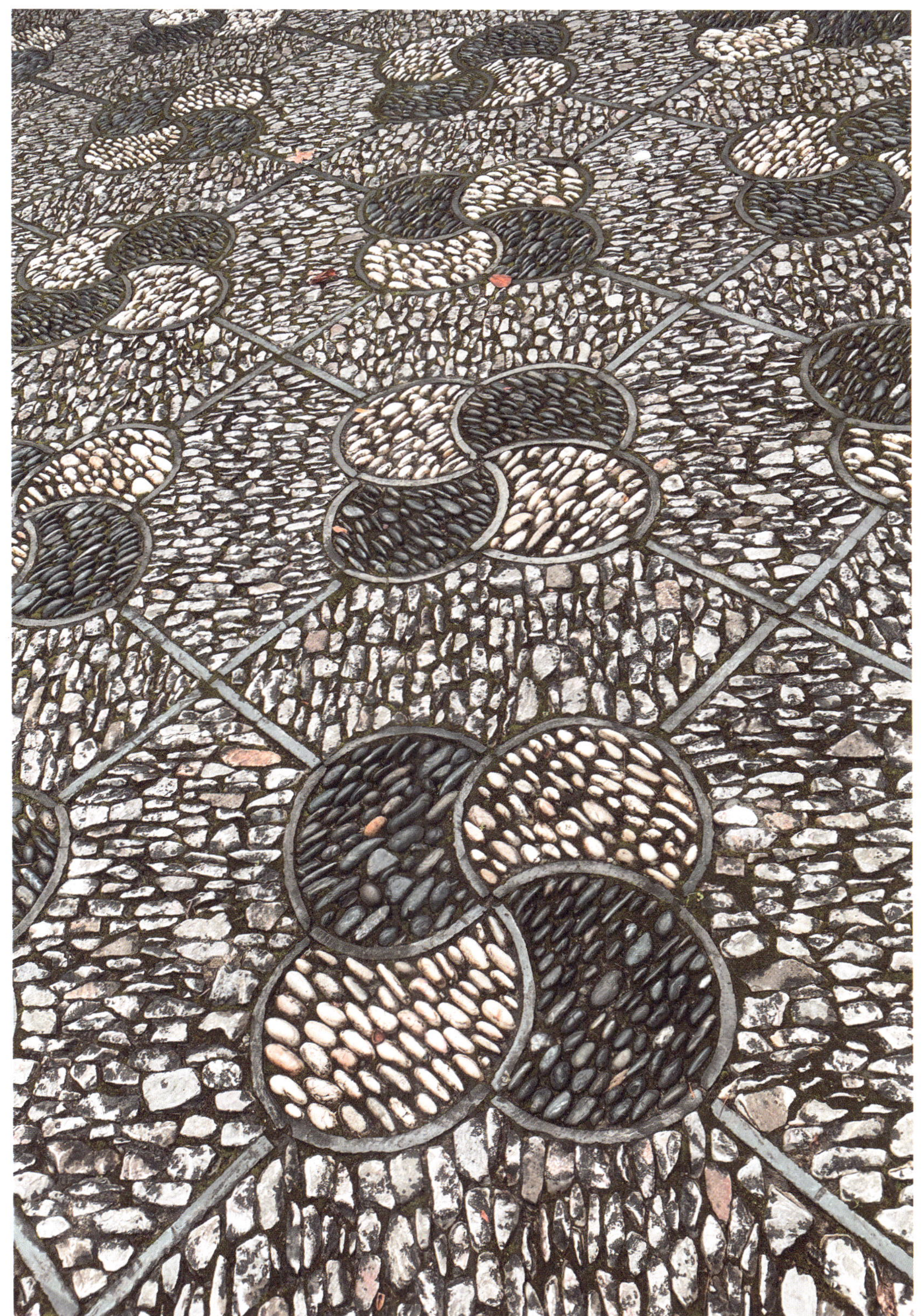

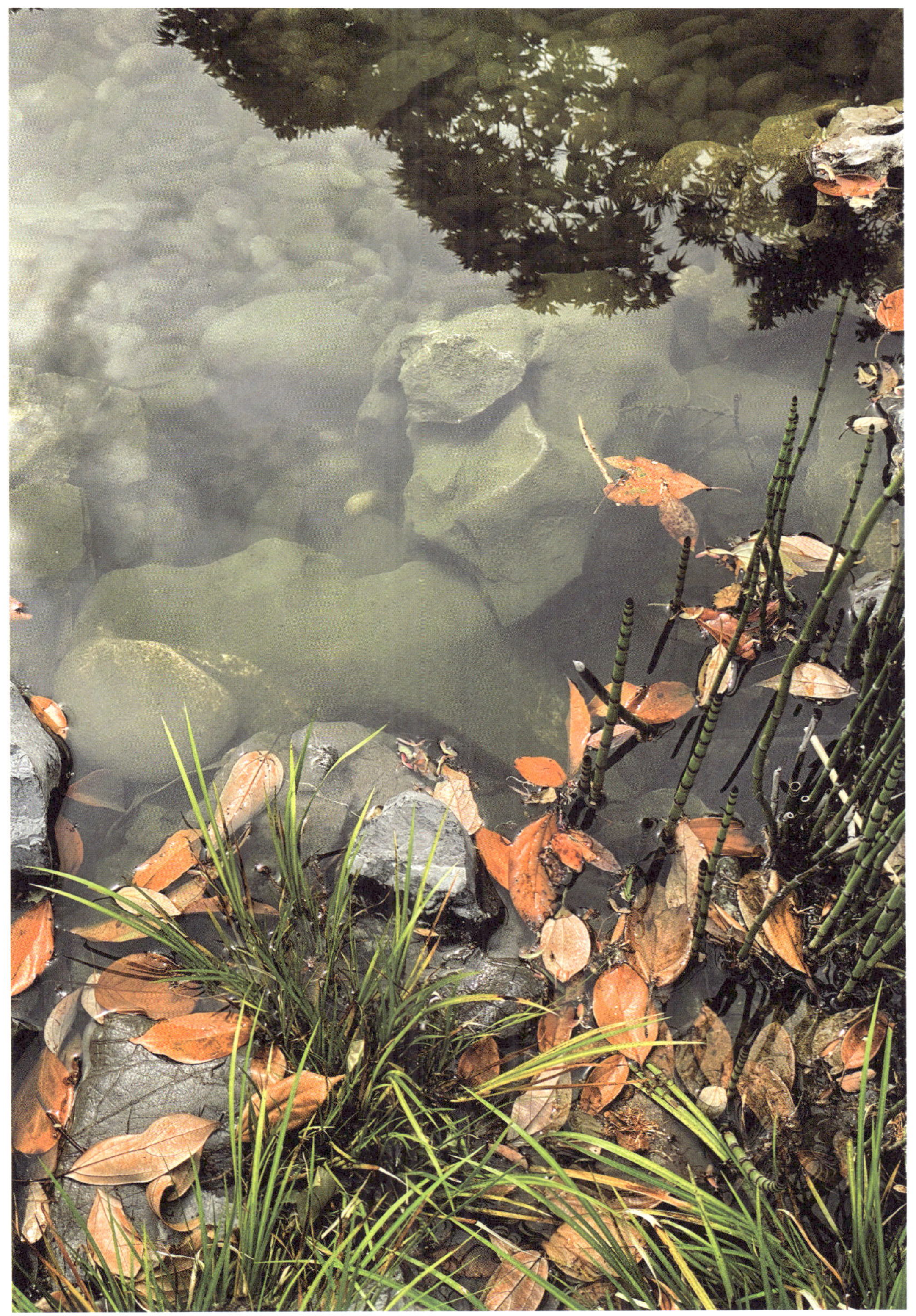

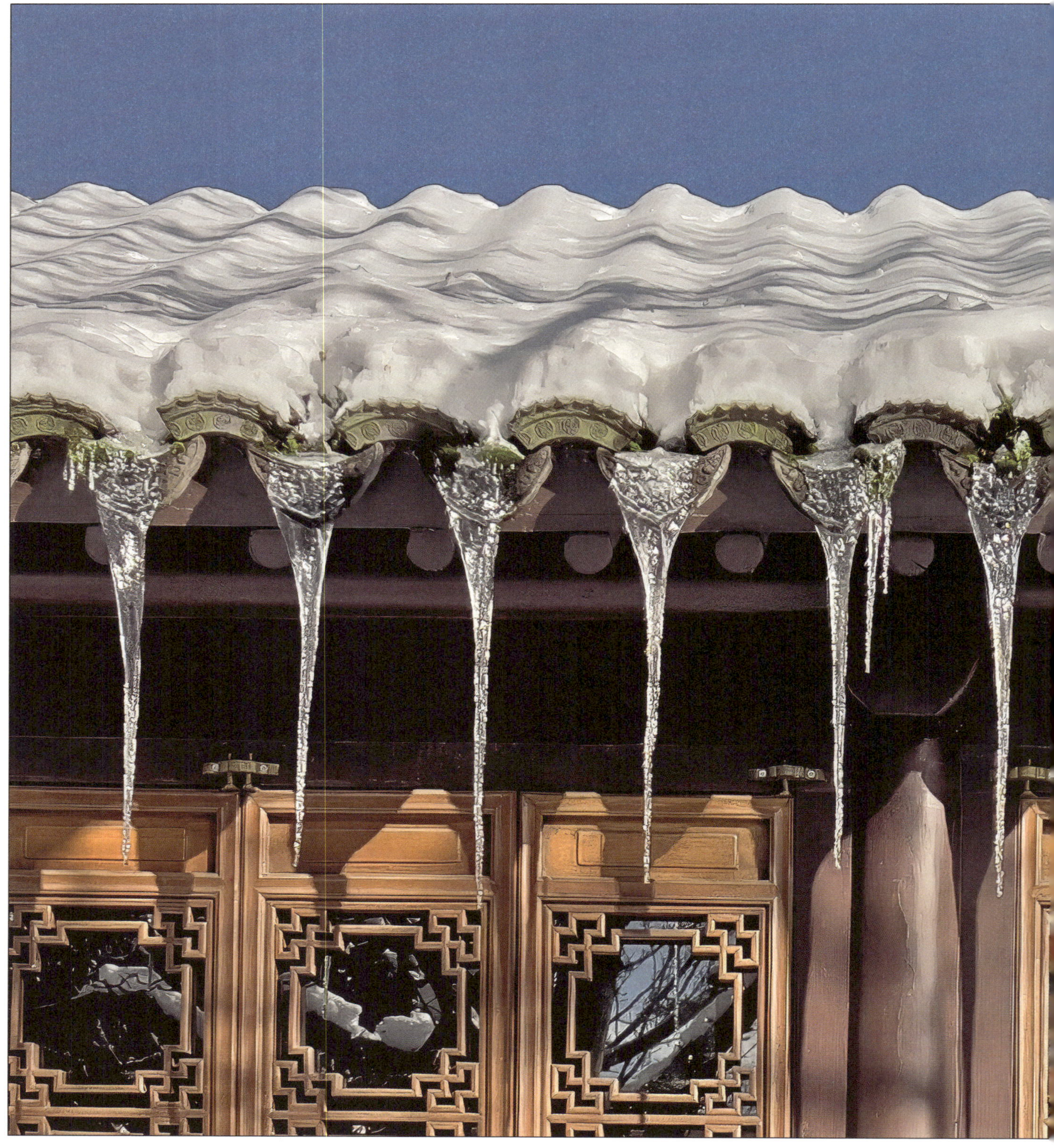

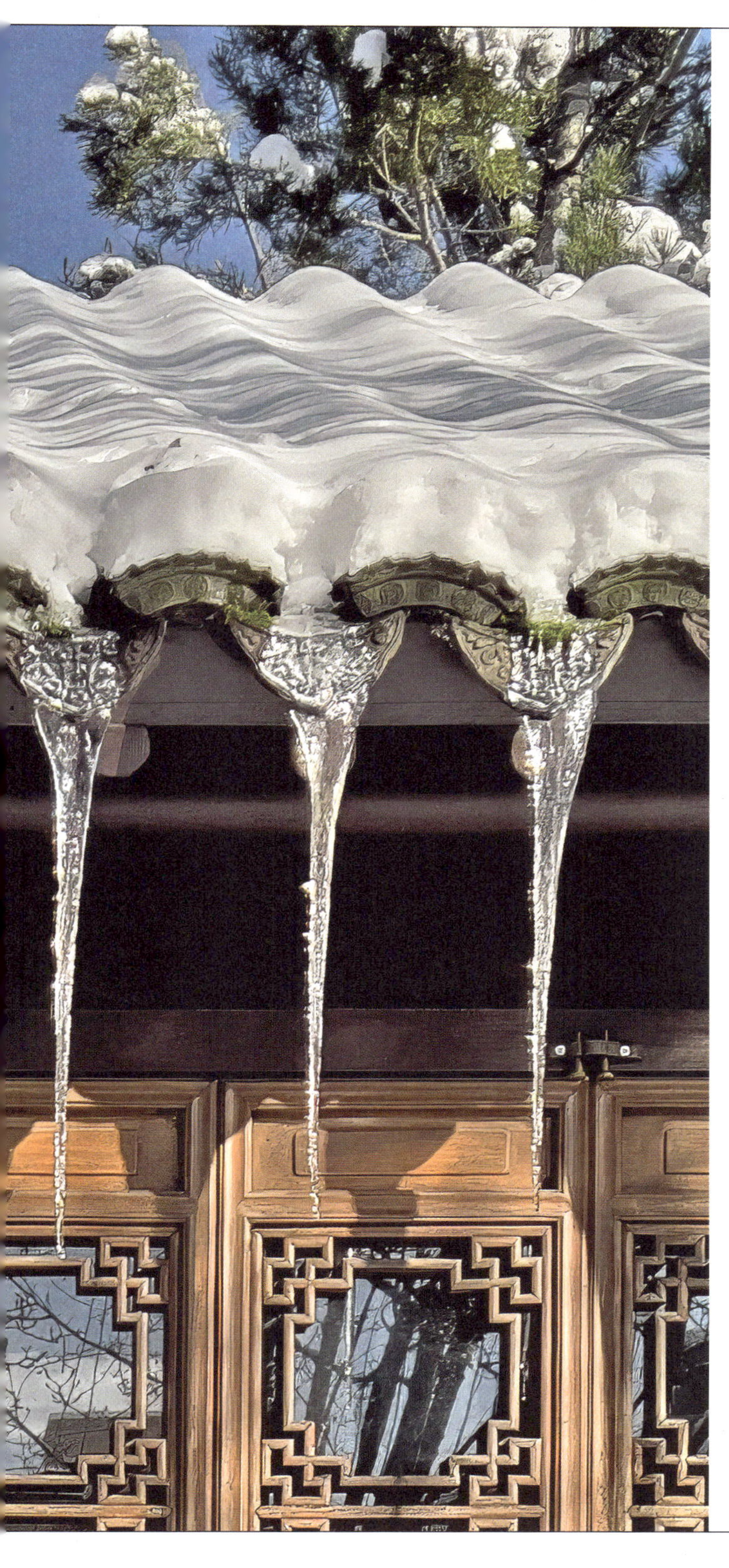

DEEP WINTER

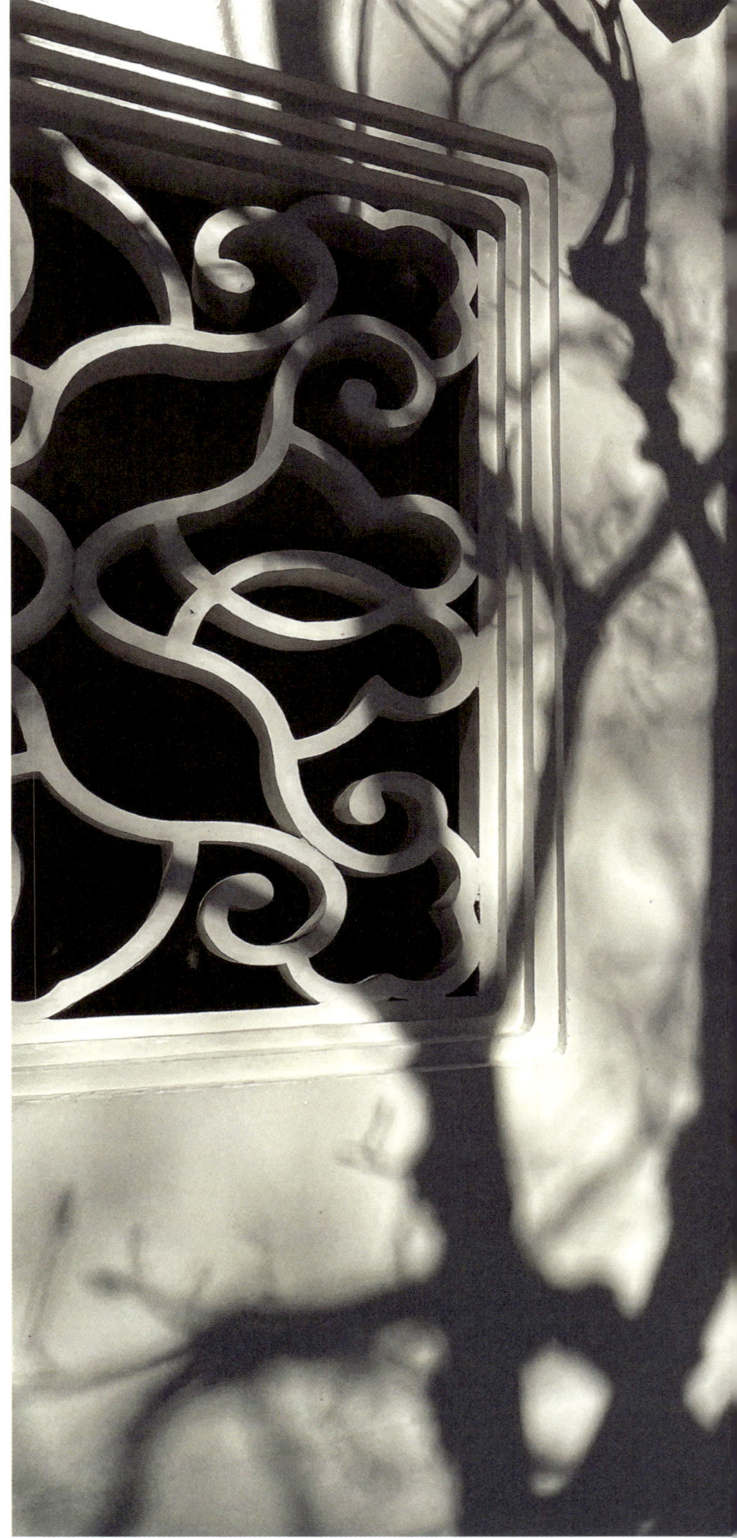

Exterior with Tree Shadows

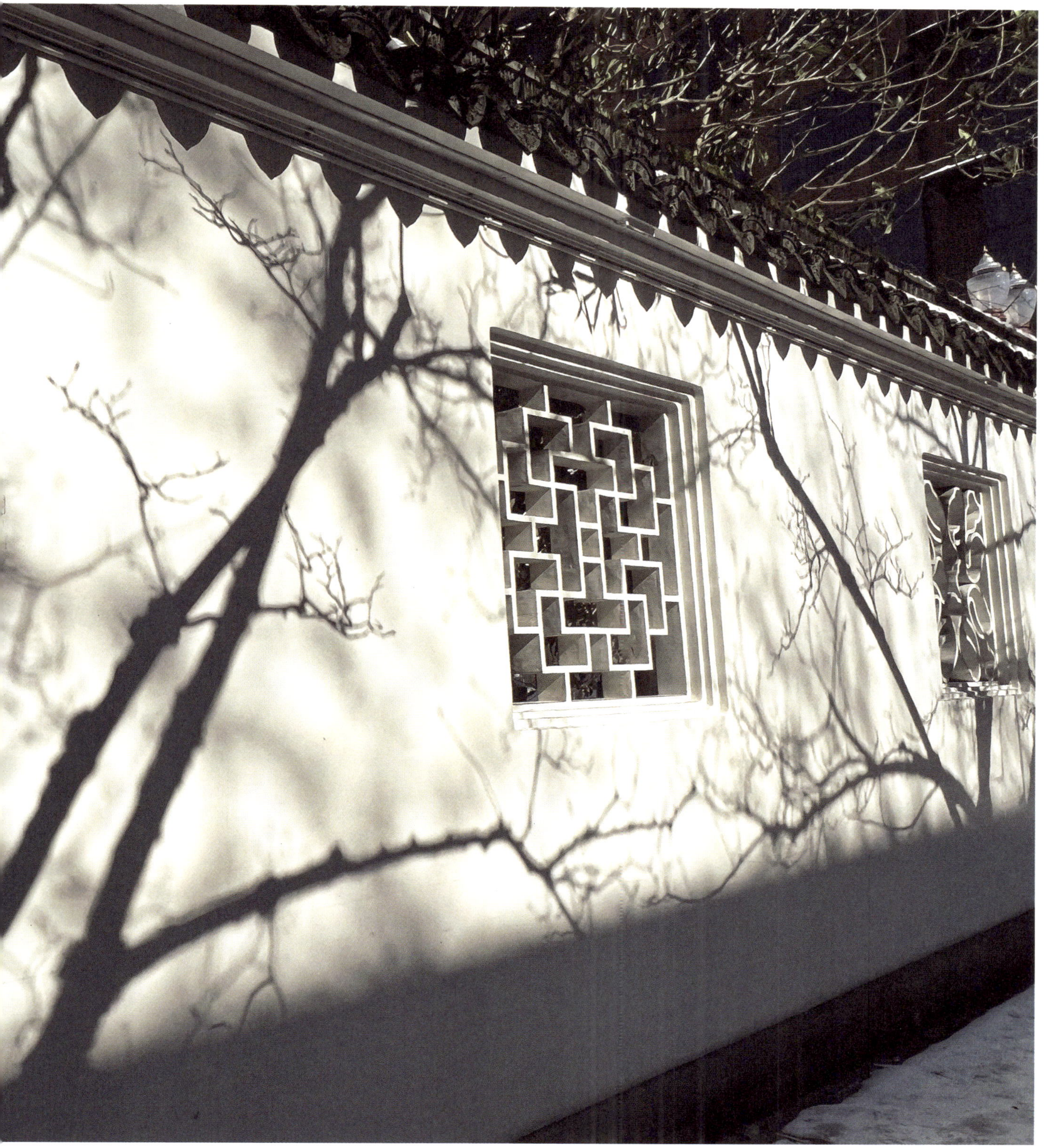

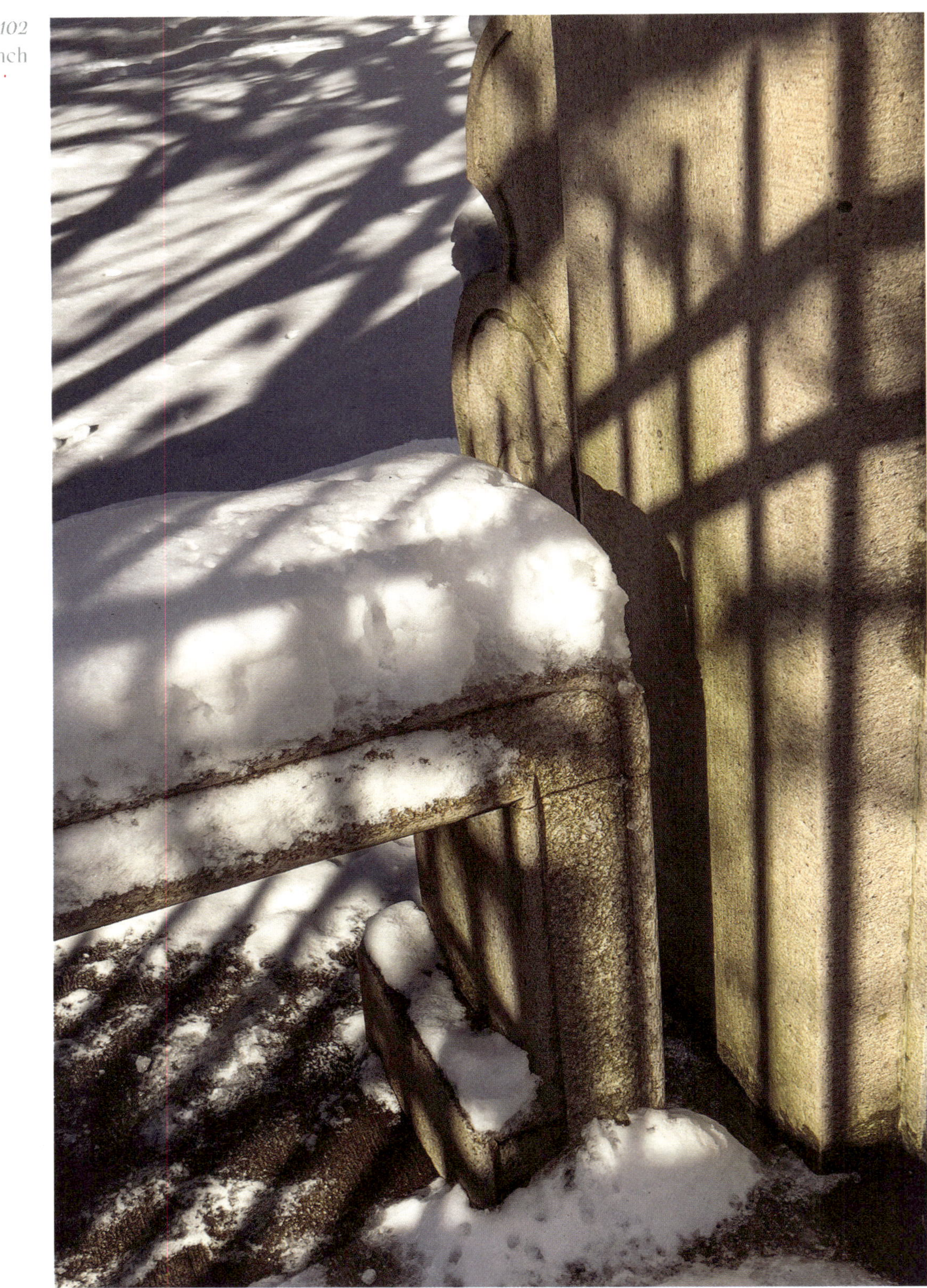

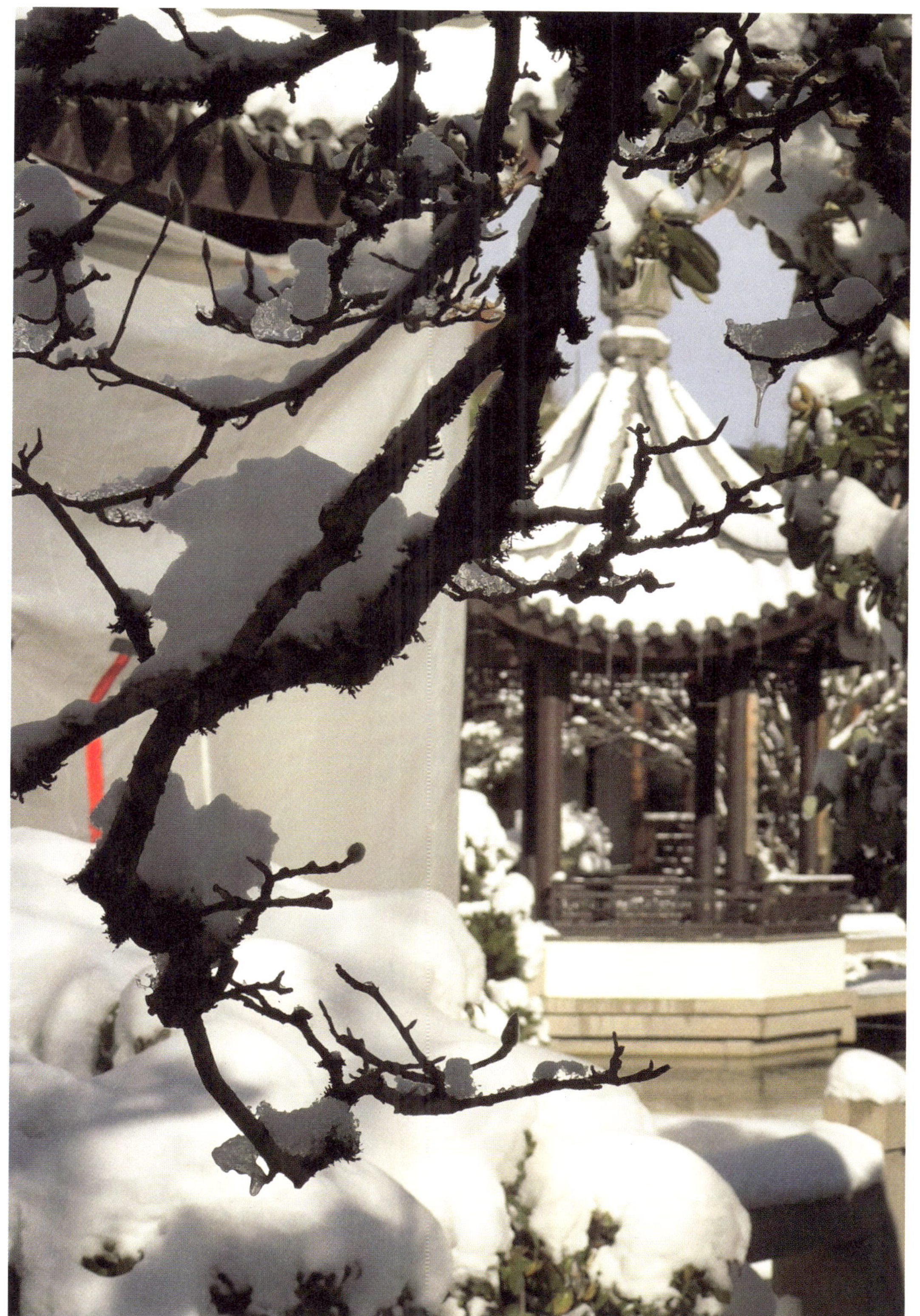

Snowy Pagoda
Ting
103

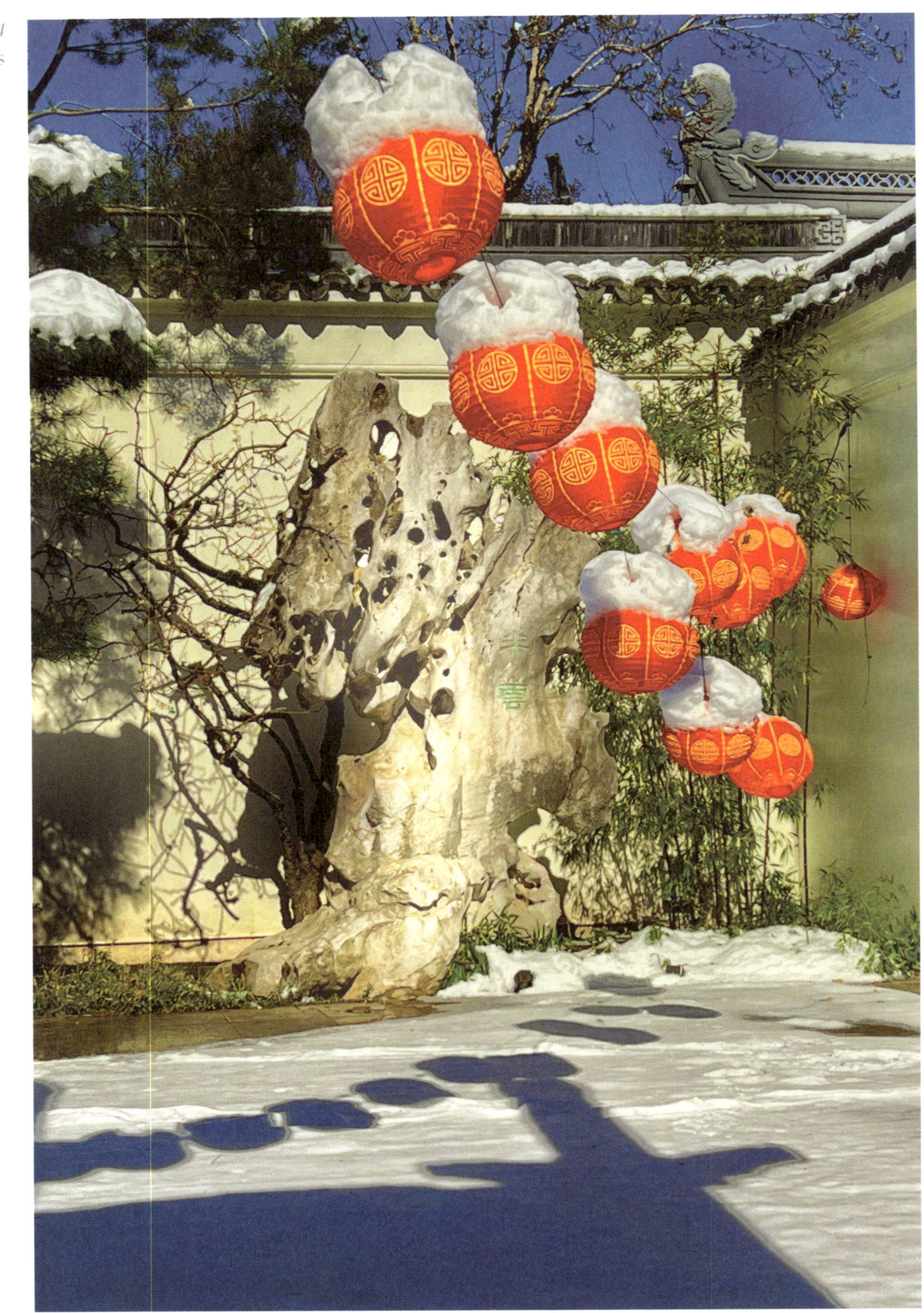

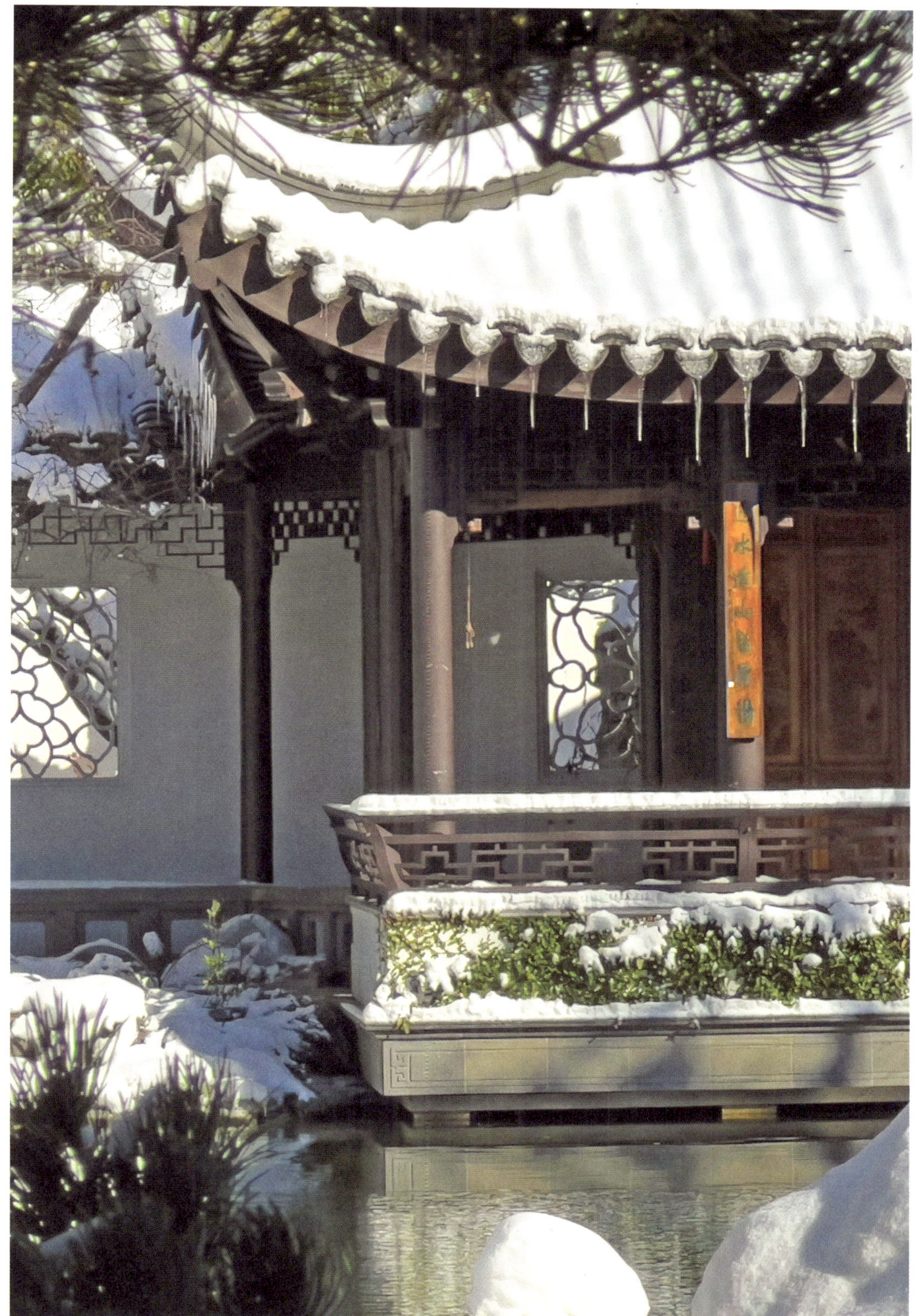

Pavillion of Flowers
Bathing in Spring Rain
(Xie)

105

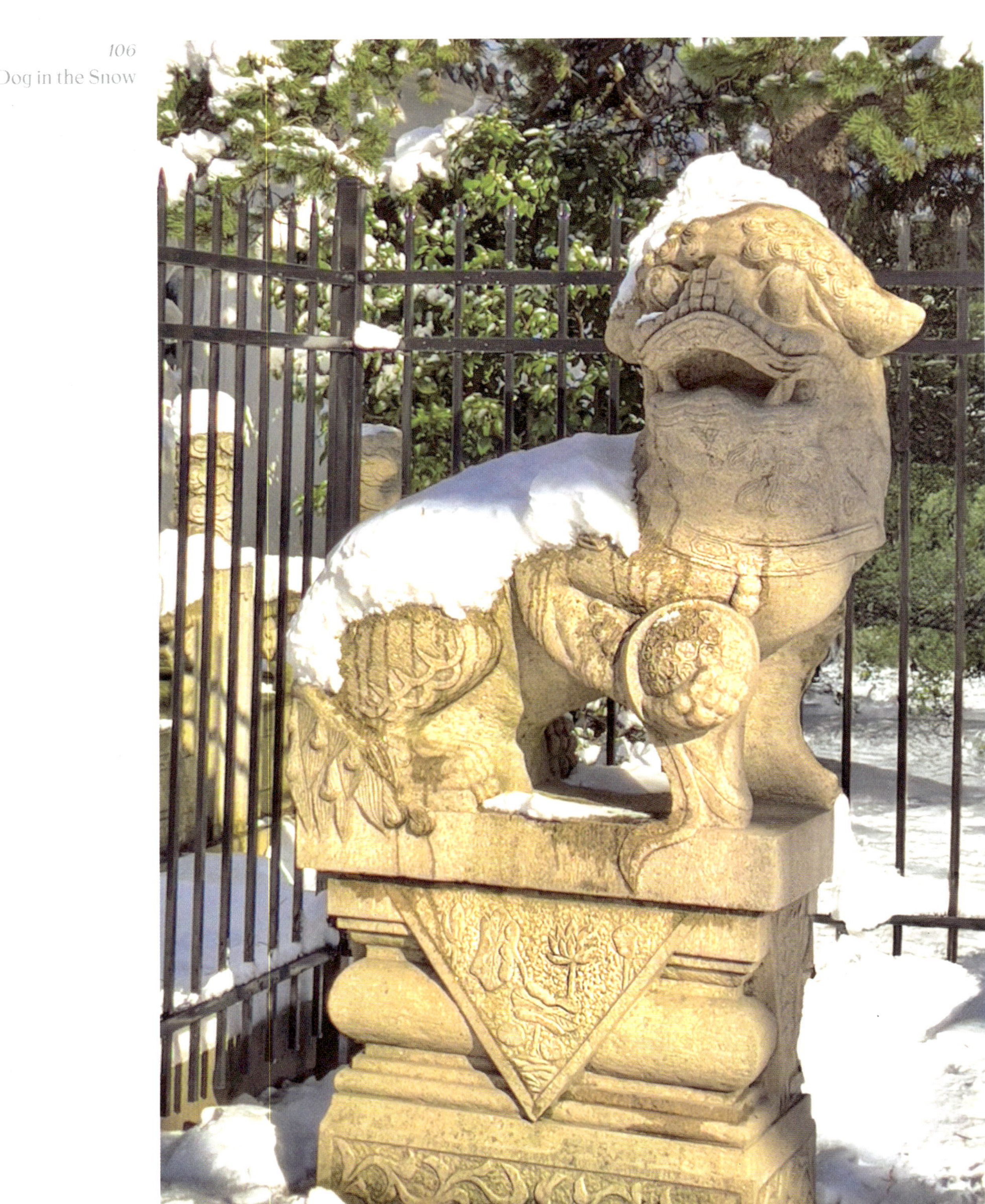

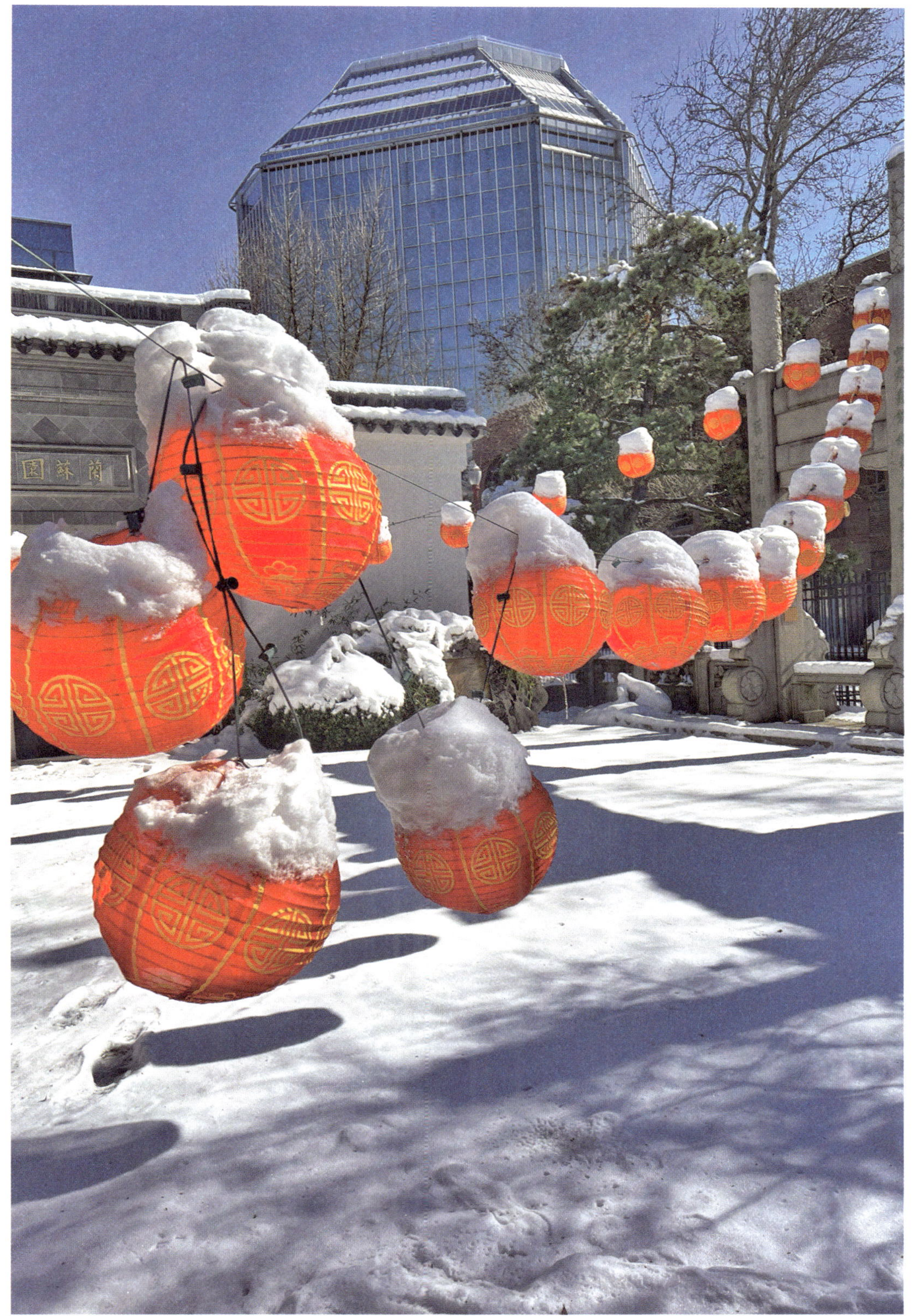

Snowy Lanterns

107

新年快樂